KNITTING MASTERCLASS

with over 20 technical workshops and 15 beautiful patterns

The **Knitter**

KNITTING MASTERCLASS

with over 20 technical workshops and 15 beautiful patterns

Edited by Juliet Bernard

COLLINS & BROWN

CONTENTS

First published in the
United Kingdom in 2013 by
Collins & Brown
10 Southcombe Street
London W14 0RA

An imprint of Anova Books Company Ltd

Copyright © Future Publishing Ltd and
Collins & Brown 2013

ISBN 978-1-90844-902-3

A CIP catalogue for this book is available from the
British Library.

10 9 8 7 6 5 4 3 2 1

Reproduction by Mission Productions Ltd, Hong Kong
Printed and bound by 1010 Printing International Ltd,
China

This book can be ordered direct from the publisher at
www.anovabooks.com

FOREWORD

The joy of knitting is that there is always something left to learn,
whether it be a clever tip passed on by a friend at your knitting
group or an unusual technique for you to try out in a pattern.

When we launched *The Knitter* in January 2009 it was always our
intention to aim our designs at the growing number of highly
accomplished knitters, wherever they happened to be in the world.
But our magazine has a greater responsibility than that. The designs
we commission, the techniques we use and the creativity of the
designers we work with are all brought together to inspire our readers.

This is why we decided to include a Masterclass in each issue of
The Knitter, so that we could help our readers to learn something new,
to develop their skills and maybe even to see their craft in a completely
new light. As knitters we are constantly learning and I hope this book
will take you a little further on your journey to becoming a master
crafts-person. I have really enjoyed revisiting our masterclasses and
choosing the projects that I hope will inspire, excite and intrigue you
as you learn.

Enjoy

Juliet Bernard
Editor, *The Knitter*

ABOUT THE MASTERS

 ## Belinda Boaden
An accomplished designer in her own right, Belinda is also pattern writer to the stars, working with many famous names to turn their ideas into completed knitting patterns.

 ## Judy Furlong
Judy's fine lace designs draw their inspiration from the traditions of Shetland. Now Judy shares her secrets to knitting perfect lace in her Masterclass. Follow her advice and you'll never tear your hair out over a missed yarn over again!

 ## Jane Crowfoot
Jane is a leading knitting expert in the UK, formerly holding the position of design consultant manager for Rowan. She has also worked closely with Debbie Bliss, and is a published author.

 ## Emma King
After developing a love of yarns while studying for her degree in textiles, Emma began knitting, and has never stopped. Her passion is for handknitted accessories, which have been the focus of three of her books to date.

 ## Annie Modesitt
Based in Minnesota, Annie is a designer and teacher. As well as being the author of several books, she is an expert on 'Combination knitting' – a style that uses elements from both Western and Eastern methods of knitting.

 ## Woolly Wormhead
Known for her architectural hat designs using innovative constructions, Woolly Wormhead is an expert on grafting techniques.

 ## Judy Becker
Judy believes that knitting is an adventure and has never met a knitting problem she didn't want to tackle. This led her to develop Judy's Magic Cast-On, a stable and invisible provisional cast-on.

ABOUT THE DESIGNERS

Kirstie McLeod

A talented designer with an expert eye for shape, fit and colour, Kirstie has had hundreds of patterns published, and has co-authored a book on socks. She is well known as the commissioning editor of *Simply Knitting* magazine.

Todd Gocken

Illinois-based designer Todd brings a fresh approach to men's knitwear, offering a range of wearable, textured designs that stand out from the crowd.

Jon Dunn-Ballam

Formerly a graphic designer, Jon creates patterns to complement the beautiful yarn he hand-dyes and sells under his Easyknits brand. His knowledge of colour and shape shines through in his striking designs.

Amanda Crawford

Since Amanda first worked in a knitwear factory, her career in the industry has developed as she went on to design for high-street stores like M&S and Principles. She has also created many lovely designs for Rowan and Patons.

Jeanette Sloan

Self-confessed accessory obsessive Jeanette has produced many modern, beautiful accessories and handbags under her design label DuppDupp. Recently she has launched her own yarn line and continues to design for some of the biggest names in the business.

Jen Arnall-Culliford

Well known to many readers as *The Knitter*'s former technical editor, Jen is now a successful tech editor and designer, working closely with the likes of Susan Crawford, Fyberspates and Jamieson & Smith on their pattern collections.

1 CHOOSING & SUBSTITUTING YARNS

As knitters we often buy patterns thinking we can use yarn from our stash, or maybe we fall in love with a yarn without knowing what to do with it. Substituting a yarn might seem quite daunting even if it is the same weight as the original. How do you know if it is the right kind of yarn and how do you know what the outcome will be? Read on for the tips and techniques you need to know to make substitution a happy marriage between yarn and pattern.

MAKING GREAT YARN CHOICES
Jane Crowfoot

YARN WEIGHTS

UK name	1ply	2ply	4ply	Baby	DK	–	Aran	Chunky	Super chunky
US name	Cobweb	Lace	Fingering	Sport	Light worsted	Worsted	Heavy worsted	Bulky	Super bulky
Also known as	–	–	Superfine, Sock or Baby	Heavy 4ply, Fine or 5ply	Light or 8ply	Heavy DK, 10ply or Afghan	10ply	12ply or Craft	Roving
Tension in st st to 10cm (sts)	–	32–34	28 is UK standard (27–32)	23–26	22 is UK standard (21–24)	20	16 is UK standard (16–18)	12–15	6–11
Usual needle size	–	1.25–3mm	2.25–3.25mm	3.25–3.75mm	3.25–4.5mm	3.75–4.5mm	5–6.5mm	5.5–8mm	9mm+

There are many reasons why you may want to change the type of yarn used to knit your chosen project. Most vintage patterns were written for yarns long since discontinued, for example. The pattern's designer may live overseas and have used a yarn from their own country, so you may need use a yarn that's available locally to you.

Other reasons may be to do with the properties of the specified yarn. For example, you may be creating a baby garment and want to choose something softer, or you may be knitting for somebody who is allergic to wool. Perhaps you don't like knitting with certain types of yarn.

To make the best yarn substitutions for your project, there are a number of important things you'll need to consider. Our guide is here to help you to make the right decisions, every time! Three main features determine the properties of a yarn: its construction, fibre content and weight.

Fibres are spun into single strands or plies of yarn. Some yarns consist of a single ply, but many are formed from a number of plies spun together. This is described as the yarn's construction. There are other ways that a single ply can be transformed into yarn, including chain constructions, but plied yarns are most commonly used.

The fibre content of a yarn falls into one of three main categories, based on its origin: animal, plant or synthetic.

Yarn weights are traditionally named according to how many plies were spun together. More plies would make a heavier-weight yarn. These days, the weight of yarn is determined by the thickness of the yarn, and what tension the yarn knits to.

Fibre content

Different fibres can have drastically different properties – think about how cashmere feels when compared with cotton. There are obvious differences in warmth and softness. But a 50g ball of DK-weight cotton will contain around 120m of yarn, where the equivalent cashmere will be around 220m. So for a similar-sized piece of knitted fabric, the cotton will be much heavier. It is important to consider these differences when making substitutions.

From left to right: Laceweight, 4ply, DK and aran yarns.

Yarn weight

To get results closest to the original pattern, you will need to substitute like with like, both in terms of weight and fibre content. The table on page 11 shows the names of different yarn weights, plus standard tension and needle size information.

It's not always clear from the name of a yarn or its ball band what weight it is. Have a look at the tension information on the ball band, and compare it to the table to find out your yarn's weight.

Tension

The tension of your knitted piece is the number of stitches and rows in a 10cm square: most patterns give details of an ideal tension, as do many yarns. It is important that you achieve the tension stated in the pattern, to ensure that your project turns out the correct size and uses the right amount of yarn.

If you can match stitch tension, but not row tension, then you may be using a yarn of slightly different thickness from the original. If you want to use a yarn that matches stitch tension, but not row tension, be aware that parts of the pattern that rely on number of rows may not turn out the correct length. If the pattern mostly relies on knitting to a particular length, it shouldn't be a problem. However, you may need to purchase extra yarn if you are working more than the specified number of rows (and less yarn if you are working fewer than the specified number of rows).

Use pins to mark out the 10cm square in the centre of your swatch before counting stitches and rows.

Thicker yarns will have fewer rows to 10cm than a finer yarn knitted to the same stitch tension, so you could look for another slightly thicker or thinner alternative.

Substituting yarn

Having decided to use a different yarn, you need to evaluate which yarn to choose. It's easiest to stick to the same weight of yarn – but even then, there are some things to bear in mind, and a few calculations which need to be made.

Working a swatch

To be sure you make the right yarn choice, work a good-sized tension sample. This will not only allow you to evaluate drape, but will also confirm whether or not your alternative achieves the same tension as the specified yarn.

Cast on enough stitches to work a generous-sized swatch – around 15cm is ideal. If the pattern gives tension information over 10cm, add half the number of stitches again to achieve a 15cm swatch.

Next, work the specified pattern repeat until you have a knitted piece that is roughly square. Cast off all stitches, and wash and block the swatch.

You are now ready to measure the tension and inspect the fabric created. Does the fabric look similar to what you're trying to achieve – dense for a coat, for example, or airy for a lacy shawl?

Try laying the swatch over your hand to look at its drape. You wouldn't usually want much drape in a jacket

or socks, but you would for an evening top or scarf. Compare our two examples: the green sample has a lot of drape, whereas the red one is much stiffer **(1)**.

Finally, examine your swatch to see whether the yarn is suitable for the technique you're using. Are colour changes even in your colourwork? Do the cables stand out enough? Is the lace pattern clear? If you're happy with the swatch, you can then calculate how much yarn is needed.

Calculating yarn amounts

A pattern will tell you how much yarn to buy for your project. If you don't use the specified yarn, then you may also have to change the amount of yarn you purchase.

To calculate how many balls you will need, work out the total length of the original yarn then divide this by the metreage of one ball of your chosen alternative.

Example: your pattern requires eight balls of a yarn with 160m per 100g ball. This means that you will need 8 x 160m = 1280m in total. Your chosen yarn comes in 80m/50g balls, so 1280 ÷ 80 = 16 balls required.

Aran swatches

We knitted swatches using three different aran-weight yarns. All were knitted using 5mm needles and have the same number of stitches and rows, but the finished effects are quite different **(2)**.

Swatch 1 (left): Manos del Uruguay Wool Clasica (Aran; 100% wool; 126m/100g). This is the largest sample. Stitch definition is acceptable and the sample feels sturdy. The slubby nature of the yarn means that there is some unevenness in the twisted stitch pattern, but its sturdiness would make it great for a jacket **(3)**.

Swatch 2 (centre): Debbie Bliss Luxury Tweed Aran (Aran; 85% wool, 15% angora; 88m/50g). The tweedy nature of this yarn disguises the stitch pattern somewhat. This sample feels a bit softer to handle than the Manos del Uruguay swatch, and comes up very slightly smaller.

Swatch 3 (right): Louisa Harding Thistle (Aran; 60% merino wool, 40% baby suri alpaca; 90m/50g). This sample

is the smallest of the three and has a nice drape to it. Unlike the Manos swatch, it feels more suited to a fine style of garment and wouldn't make a hardwearing outer-wear garment. The slight halo of the yarn softens the twisted stitch pattern.

DK swatches

Our two swatches **(4)** were knitted using 4mm needles.

Swatch 1 (left): Sirdar Snuggly Baby Bamboo (DK; 80% bamboo, 20% wool; 95m/50g). This has excellent drape and a subtle sheen. Knitting a colourwork pattern in this yarn is tricky, and there are some areas of uneven tension because the yarn is smooth and slippery **(5)**.

Swatch 2 (right): Rowan Wool Cotton (DK; 50% merino wool, 50% cotton; 113m/50g). The stitch definition here is slightly better, and the presence of the wool makes the yarn more forgiving in the colourwork pattern. The row tension on this swatch is closer to that specified in the pattern.

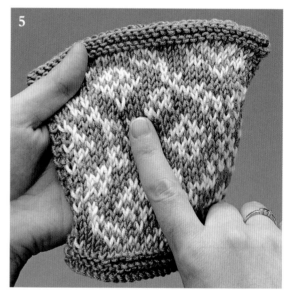

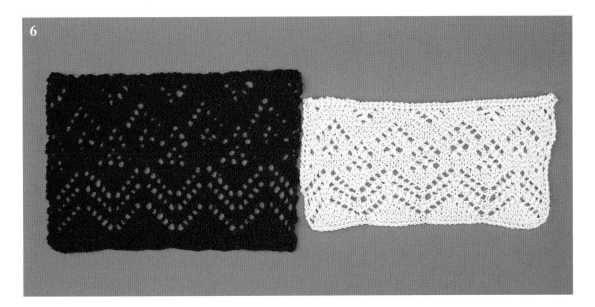

6

Lace swatches

Our two swatches (6) were knitted on 3.25mm needles, then washed and blocked.

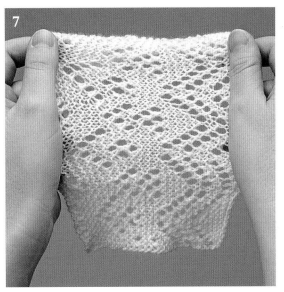

7

Swatch 1 (left): Jamieson & Smith Lace 2ply (Lace; 100% Shetland wool; 169m/25g). This gives a really crisp finish. It blocks beautifully and holds its shape, helping the lace pattern to stand out really well.

Swatch 2 (right): Sirdar Snuggly 2ply (Lace; 55% nylon, 45% acrylic; 462m/50g). The stitch definition in this smooth nylon–acrylic blend laceweight is excellent. However, it doesn't hold its blocked shape for very long, so the lace pattern doesn't show up nearly as well (7).

We hope we've shown that knitting swatches is well worth the time and effort when making any yarn substitution. The yarns that didn't work so well in our samples will be perfect for other patterns, so a good supply of odd balls of yarn can always come in handy.

ALTERING PATTERNS TO WORK WITH ALTERNATIVE YARNS

Belinda Boaden

The challenge

Every knitter knows this feeling. You see a pattern you know you have to cast on immediately, but a trip to your local yarn shop is out of the question, and you think, 'I must have something I can use'. A quick flick through the stash yields incompatible yarn, however. Or does it? Can you really knit a design written up for aran-weight yarn in DK or even 4ply?

As ever, the answer is 'yes, depending'. With a willingness to swatch and do a few calculations this may seem daunting, but it doesn't have to be traumatic!

First steps

First of all, consider the yarn the pattern is written for and the yarn you wish to knit it up in. Certainly if it's your first venture off-piste, then aim to keep within the same fibre family, as that will help to give you a garment looking and behaving the same way as the sample – a wool-based yarn for another wool-based yarn, for example (as opposed to a cotton or viscose).

Also don't try to work with a substitute yarn that is hugely different in weight – aran to DK is not too much of a leap, but aran to 4ply might be a step too far for a first attempt at yarn substitution.

Second, consider exactly what you need to do. If it seems just too onerous a task, then go and buy new yarn. Substituting will take effort if you want to be sure of a decent garment, and it's not wrong or bad to decide that you don't want to bother. What is soul destroying is to start, then get discouraged, not finish it or (even worse) hate what you end up with.

The swatch

Knit a reasonably large swatch in your new yarn in the stitch pattern called for in the tension section of the pattern. If it's your first go at substituting, pick a pattern that is fairly basic (in terms of shape and stitch patterns used) until you're confident of your ability to do all the maths.

Here we're going to substitute Rowan Felted Tweed DK for Shilasdair Luxury DK. Although the Shilasdair is called a DK, it's thicker than the Felted Tweed and knitted at a tension of 18 sts and 24 rows to 10cm in stocking stitch on 5mm needles. The Felted Tweed, on the other hand, has a recommended tension on the ball band of 22–24 sts and 30–32 rows to 10cm on 3.75mm or 4mm needles **(1)**.

Knit your swatch so that you have a fabric quality you like and then measure your tension after steaming or wet blocking (whatever your preference is).

Our swatch of Felted Tweed is 40 stitches and 50 rows knitted on 4mm needles with a tension after a good steam of 21 stitches and 28 rows to 10cm. This is slightly looser than the ball band recommends, but we like the fabric quality so will go with it **(2)**.

A note on swatch size – a decent-sized swatch helps here for two reasons. First, you can get a really accurate measurement over 10cm as you're not relying on (possibly) wobbly edge stitches when you're counting. Also, it will help to confirm roughly how much of your subbed yarn you're going to need to finish your project.

Working out how much yarn you will need is perhaps the trickiest part of substituting. The best thing to do is to weigh your swatch as accurately as possible and work out

its total area. As mentioned on the previous pages, you can estimate by metreage but for accuracy when changing weights, weigh your swatch on electronic scales.

If you can draw out your spec to scale on graph paper, you can then work out roughly how many times your swatch would fit into the back of the garment, double this to account for the front and carry out the same process with the sleeve spec. It's a good idea to add on 10% or so to cover wastage and sewing up.

The measurements

Let's say we're going to rework the pattern for size 10. Sometimes the flat spec drawing given with the pattern will have all the information on it that you need; more often it won't and you'll have to work backwards from stitch counts within the pattern to get all the measurements needed.

The blocking diagram given with the pattern here has only three measurements on it: bust, total length and sleeve seam length. These are not enough to work from; what we really need are the measurements shown in figures **3** and **4**.

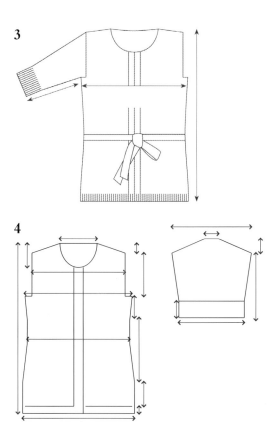

Our example swaps a heavy DK yarn, shown in the garment above, for a light DK yarn.

This looks quite daunting, but not all of these measurements will need to be worked out. Some are given in the pattern (usually lengths), so go through the written instructions and add onto your diagram any lengths given for your size **(5)**. The pattern here gives lengths for where the waist shaping begins so these are added in; also, although some lengths are not given they can be worked out – the shoulder shaping depth, for example (d). The pattern gives us the total length of the cardigan (a) and also the length to the underarm (b) plus the length of the armhole (c), so take (b) and (c) from (a) and you're left with (d). This is the point at which to alter any of these lengths to fit you personally.

Now for the width measurements. First, you need to know how many stitches to cast on. Size 10 has 87 stitches cast on in the Shilasdair yarn, which at the given tension of 18 stitches to 10cm gives a width of:

$$87 \text{ (sts)} \div 18 \text{ (sts to 10cm)} = 4.83 \times 10 \text{ (cm)} = 48.3\text{cm}$$

You can keep or leave the 3mm depending on personal preference at this point. If you're being really accurate leave it in, but it's not going to be the end of the world if you drop it.

The waist decreases have you decrease down to 79 sts, giving a measurement of:

$$79 \div 18 = 4.38 \times 10 = 43.8\text{cm}$$

And then you increase back up to 85 sts for the bust:

$$85 \div 18 = 4.72 \times 10 = 47.2\text{cm}$$

After the armhole cast offs you're left with 73 sts for the chest:

$$73 \div 18 = 4.05 \times 10 = 40.5\text{cm}$$

The easiest way to work out the shoulder measurements is to see how many stitches you have for the back neck – 27 here – and then work out that width:

$$27 \div 18 = 1.5 \times 10 = 15\text{cm}$$

And then use this measurement to work out each shoulder width:

$$40.5 - 15 = 25.5 \div 2 = 12.75\text{cm}$$ for each shoulder width (chest measurement – back neck measurement ÷ 2 = shoulder width)

Write these measurements onto your spec **(6)**.

Now work out your DK stitches required to arrive at the same measurements:

$$48.3 \div 10 = 4.83 \times 21 \text{ (new stitch tension to 10cm taken from your swatch)} = 101.43$$

So you would be casting on 101 stitches instead of 79 – quite a difference.

Work out your other new stitch requirements and write them onto your spec **(7)**. Here you need to make sure that if you start with an even (or odd) number of stitches you need to decrease down to an even (or odd) number of stitches at the waist and back to an even (or odd) number at the bust, so stitch counts may need a stitch gaining or dropping to keep the decreases/increases even on both sides (seen here at the waist after the decreases – you should have 91.98 stitches which normally would be rounded up to 92, but as you need an odd number here it's better to round down to 91).

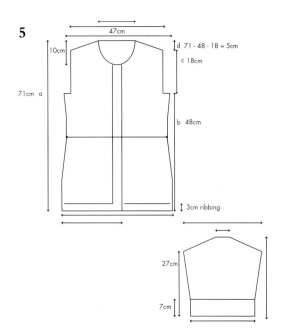

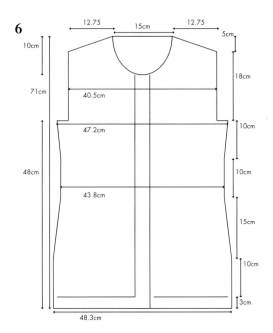

Shoulder shaping is where row tension becomes important. You need to decrease the 27 stitches for each shoulder over 5cm, which equates to 14 rows in total. So you would cast off: 54 ÷ 14 = 3.86 sts per row **(8)**.

This is obviously not viable, so decrease:

12 x 4 = 48 sts

2 x 3 = 6 sts

48 + 6 = 54 sts (27 sts per shoulder).

Row tension is also important for working out the spacing between waist shaping increases/decreases and also sleeve shaping. With all the measurements and stitch counts for the body on your spec, it's easy then to work out that you have to decrease 5 stitches each side of the body for the waist shaping and that you have 15cm/42 rows to do this in:

15 (length in cm) ÷ 10 (cm) x 28 (number of rows to 10cm) = 42 rows

So assuming you would decrease right at the beginning and as close to the end of the 42 rows as possible, decrease 1 stitch at each end of the first row, then every following 10th row, making your last decrease on row 41 of the 42 **(9)**.

The front pieces would be worked out in exactly the same way – because you have all of the lengths and shaping needed, the only calculations needed are for the cast on number of stitches, and allowing for a couple of extra stitches, perhaps, in the twisted rib bands.

The neck shaping might be slightly more complicated. As you know the number of stitches required for the shoulder, the remainder of the stitches need to be decreased away for the neck in a pleasing curve, but once you've knitted the back it should be easy to get an idea from looking at that how many stitches to cast off per row.

The same principles apply to the sleeves. Work out your width from the original number of stitches cast on, and convert this to stitches in your new yarn. Work out the width after the sleeve increases and convert this to stitches in your subbed yarn. Now you know how many stitches you need to increase and you can work out how many rows you have to fit these increases into from the total length to the beginning of the sleevehead decreases minus the length of the ribbing (20cm here – 56 rows). Your sleevehead decreases are worked over 12 rows in the original pattern – 5cm, so need to be worked over 14 rows.

And there you have it. The amount of work you need to put in will be directly influenced by how the original pattern was written, so perhaps choose your pattern carefully if it's your first try at substituting. Independent designers often include more information in their pattern than larger publishers or yarn companies, so it might be worth looking for something on the internet as your first substituting project.

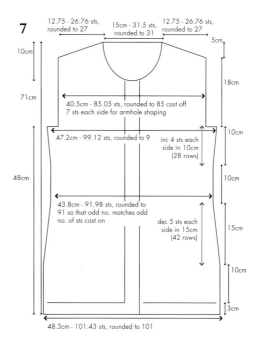

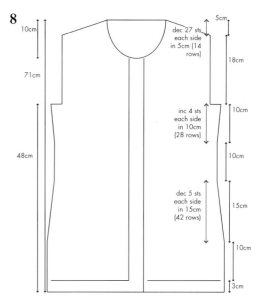

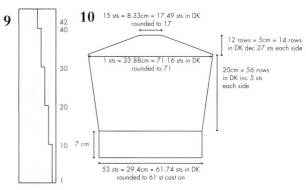

YARN SUBSTITUTION IN CABLE PATTERNS
Belinda Boaden

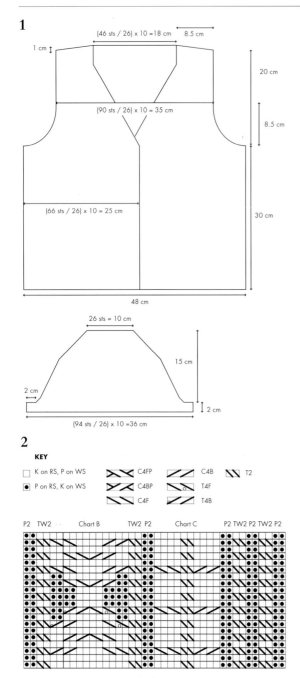

1

(46 sts / 26) x 10 = 18 cm   8.5 cm

1 cm

20 cm

(90 sts / 26) x 10 = 35 cm

8.5 cm

(66 sts / 26) x 10 = 25 cm

30 cm

48 cm

26 sts = 10 cm

15 cm

2 cm

2 cm

(94 sts / 26) x 10 = 36 cm

2

KEY

☐ K on RS, P on WS
● P on RS, K on WS

C4FP
C4BP
C4F

C4B
T4F
T4B

T2

P2   TW2   Chart B   TW2 P2   Chart C   P2 TW2 P2 TW2 P2

The cable pattern on the Sedgemoor Cardigan consists of
two main cables edged with a twisted rib, and a further
cable panel on the lower borders.

Now let's consider substituting yarns when a cabled
pattern is involved. This can involve quite complex
reworking of designs.

We'll be looking at Amanda Crawford's Sedgemoor
Cardigan (see page 24) originally knitted in Debbie Bliss
Fez on 4.5mm needles with a given tension of 26 stitches
to 10cm measured over pattern. We're going to look at
substituting two different Rowan yarns: Alpaca Chunky
and Kid Classic. The Alpaca is much chunkier than the
Fez when knitted up; the Kid Classic not as bulky.

Initial swatches

First of all we need to start exactly as we did with the plain
garment in the Altering Patterns section on page 16 –
adding to the spec drawing as published with all possible
measurements on it worked out from the pattern. Here
we're planning to knit the size 14 garment, so all
measurements are taken/worked out as detailed on page 17.
The width measurements on the 'across chest' (above the
armhole decreases on the body), back neck and the bottom
of the sleeve are a guess because the tension for the pattern
doesn't say exactly which set of pattern stitches the 26
stitches to 10cm is measured over, but this just means that
you can make these measurements your own so that you
get a great fit. Here we've worked them out assuming the
26 sts to10cm is an average for all the patterns (**1**).

Now let's work out what we need to swatch. There are
two main cable panels in Sedgemoor, panels B and C plus
a supplemental cable, panel A, which appears in the lower
borders and leads into cable B. There is also a 'filler' stitch
of a 2x2 rib variant where the two knit stitches are twisted
on every RS row (**2**).

We need to swatch all of these stitches to see how they
will appear in the new yarn and to work out tension for
the garment, so let's set up a swatch of 40 stitches.

Here we have the Alpaca Chunky swatch knitted up
on 10mm needles (**3**). This gives a lovely fabric, but the
scale of the cables is quite altered and this swatch itself is
huge – the 40 stitches here measure 26cm.

As a contrast, the Kid Classic swatch is more delicate,
giving a width of 13cm on 4mm needles (**4**). The
recommended needle size on the ball band is 5-5.5mm,

but the fabric felt thin and without the body required for cables, so we dropped to 4mm and the resulting fabric is lovely. This just shows how difficult tension can be – one yarn works beautifully with the recommendations on the ball band while one doesn't, despite being knitted by the same knitter on the same day.

Stitch counts

Now to work out how many stitches we need in our new garment. First, measure the width of your individual cable panels.

With the Alpaca Chunky cable panel B (16 sts including the 2 twisted sts either side of it) measures 11cm, panel C (10 sts) is 7.5cm and 10 sts of the twisted rib are 7cm, making each 2-st section average out at 1.4cm (7 ÷ 10 x 2 = 1.4) **(5)**.

With Kid Classic we have panel B measuring 5cm, panel C 4cm and the 10 sts of Twisted Rib 3.5cm, giving an average 2-st section a width of 0.7cm (3.5 ÷ 10 x 2 = 0.7) **(6)**.

Now, as we want to produce a chart for a size 14 garment from both of these yarns, we need to see how we can fit the cables into the width of the back. It's obvious that the Alpaca Chunky will look quite different from the original Fez garment, but the Kid Classic one perhaps not quite so much.

Using the pattern repeat of alternating panels of C and B with purl stitches and the twisted rib between **(7, page 23)**, and writing in the actual widths of each panel from our swatch, it's obvious that this will need quite serious alteration for the Alpaca Chunky as this basic repeat comes out to 53.6cm – that's 5.6cm wider than we need our size 14 back to be. The reverse is true for the Kid Classic, as the panel would be far too narrow at 25.8cm.

Working on the Alpaca Chunky first, it's easy to see that we need to rearrange stitch panels to come up with a narrower back. This is where the garment might end up more an 'inspired by' rather than a straight reworking of Sedgemoor. Basically we either need to lose two of the repeats of panel B and replace them with either extra repeats of C, or simply more 'filler' stitch of twisted rib.

Let's try getting rid of the two extra repeats of panel B and filling in with extra repeats of panel C **(7b)**. Looks good, but by the time you've added in the purl stitch columns needed to balance the cable panels, it's even wider than the original plan at 55cm, so that's no good.

The other alternative, using the filler of twisted rib shown in **7c**, comes out to 48.4cm, which is close enough. Whether it's the look you might have been hoping for is another matter. This would be easy enough to use for the rest of the garment, though – the fronts could have a single panel of B and C and the appropriate filler stitches between **(7d)** and come to a width of 25.5cm, which would give the slight overlap for a button/buttonhole band.

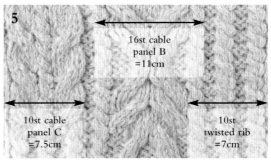

Having worked out the number of stitches to cast on for the back, we need to work out the number of stitches to cast off for the armhole shaping. This requires a little backwards-working from the spec, your stitch plan and your tension swatch.

The back needs to measure 35cm across after the armhole shapings. Working from the measurements shown on **5**, page 21, we can calculate this to be 48 sts (shown between red lines on **7c**). So our decreases need to be:

68 − 48 = 20 sts total to dec = 10 sts each side

10 − 3 (immediate cast off sts) = 7 sts

Calculating from the original pattern, the armhole decreases were worked over a total of 24 rows = 8.5cm. This equates to 12 rows in the Alpaca Chunky. So we can decrease 1 st at each end of the next 3 rows and then on every RS row until we get to the required 48 sts.

As the back neck measurement needs to be 18cm, this works out to 24 sts (shown between blue lines on **7c**), giving:

48 − 24 = 24 ÷ 2 = 12 sts for each shoulder

As the original design only had 1cm of shoulder shaping, we will cast off 6 sts at the beginning of the 4 rows after the armhole depth is reached and then cast off the remaining 24 sts.

Sleeve workings

Working out the width of the sleeve bottom using the 26 sts/10cm tension from the original (Fez) cast on stitches of 94 gives a width of 36cm, which seems a little wide looking at the photograph. This width matters: we know the total length of the sleeve is 17cm (see workings on **8**), so if we follow that length but the sleeve is too wide to start with, the chances are that the sleevehead will be too big to fit neatly into the armhole, as is actually the case here. It's easy to check this if you draw your specs out to scale on squared paper. Once you've done that use the pencil-and-edge-of-paper technique to check the actual length of both armhole and sleevehead and then adjust the sleevehead appropriately, remembering that it doesn't need to be millimetre perfect.

If you're new to the pencil-and-edge-of-paper technique, here's how to do it. Mark the distance to be covered by holding the edge of a piece of paper next to it. Using a pencil, mark the start and end point of the required measurement. This can now be used to check other aspects of the garment (e.g. sleevehead) which you've already drawn to scale.

This gives us a cast on of 42 sts (**7**). The 2cm of depth before beginning the shaping is only 3 rows here, which we will round up to 4. We know that our sleevehead needs to be 15cm deep, which equals 22 rows in the Alpaca Chunky [(15 ÷ 10) x 14].

42 sts − (2 x 3 sts) = 36 sts

We need to end up with approximately 8cm at the top of the sleevehead, which we can work out to 12 sts:

C cable panel = 10 sts and 7.5cm wide, plus 1 st either side to make things look neat.

36 − 12 = 24 sts to decrease over 20 rows, which is basically 12 actual decrease rows (24 ÷ 2 = 12). So, dec:

1 st at each end of next 5 rows and then on every RS row until 12 sts remain, cast off.

The decreases on the fronts are as for the back for the armhole (10 sts) and shoulder (12 sts), leaving 22 sts (44 − 22) to decrease for the neck, and they start on the same row as the armhole decreases. If you decrease every row, there will be some straight rows at the top of the neck after the decreases have ended, giving a nice line to the neck.

For the collar, you'll need to pick up a repeat of 4 + 2 sts around the neck to work the twisted rib pattern. You can work out how many stitches to pick up by measuring the length you need to pick up over and then dividing this by the stitch tension of your twisted rib swatch. Once you've got this figure, you can alter it slightly to fit the pattern repeat. Shaping the collar should be fairly easy to work out when you have your required stitch totals by referring to the original pattern and the picture.

Exactly the same steps are followed for substituting the Kid Classic, with stitch totals being shown on **9**. As you can see by comparing the two sets of illustrations, though, the two garments will look quite different!

BASIC CABLE LAYOUT AS ORIGINAL SEDGEMOOR

| T2 | B | T2 | P2 | C | P2 | T2 | B | T2 | P2 | C | P2 | T2 | B | T2 |

1.4   1.4   1.4   1.4

←— 11 cm —→ — 7.5 cm — ←— 11 cm —→ — 7.5 cm — ←— 11 cm —→

= 53.6 cm

7b: FIRST ALTERED LAYOUT WITH EXTRA PANELS OF C

| P2 | T2 | P2 | C | P2 | C | P2 | T2 | B | T2 | P2 | C | P2 | C | P2 | T2 | P2 |

1.4   7.5 cm   1.4   1.4   7.5 cm   1.4

←— 4.2 —→ 7.5 cm   ←— 11 cm —→   7.5 cm   ←— 4.2 —→

= 55 cm

7c: SECOND ALTERED LAYOUT TO GET DESIRED WIDTH

←— 2.8 —→   Across chest - 48 sts   ←— 2.8 —→

| P2 | T2 | P2 | T2 | P2 | T2 | P2 | C | P2 | T2 | B | T2 | P2 | C | P2 | T2 | P2 | T2 | P2 | T2 | P2 |

7.5 cm 1.4   1.4 7.5 cm

←————— 9.8 cm —————→   ←— 11 cm —→   ←————— 9.8 cm —————→

= 48.4 cm, cast on 68 sts.

Back neck - 24 sts - include 2 sts from each C panel

7d: FRONT LAYOUT

| P2 | C | P2 | T2 | B | T2 | P2 | T2 | P2 | Right front shown,
                                              with this edge
1.4 7.5 cm 1.4   ←— 11 cm —←— 2.8 —→   being the CF

= 25.5 cm, cast on 44 sts.

7e: SLEEVE LAYOUT

| P4 | T2 | P2 | T2 | P2 | T2 | P2 | T2 | P2 | C | P2 | T2 | P2 | T2 | P2 | T2 | P2 | T2 | P4 |

7.5 cm

←————— 14 cm —————→   ←————— 14c m —————→

= 35.5 cm, cast on 50 sts.

7f: REVISED SLEEVE LAYOUT

| P4 | T2 | P2 | T2 | P2 | T2 | P2 | C | P2 | T2 | P2 | T2 | P2 | T2 | P4 |

7.5 cm

←———— 12 cm ————→   ←———— 12 cm ————→

= 31.5 cm, cast on 42 sts.

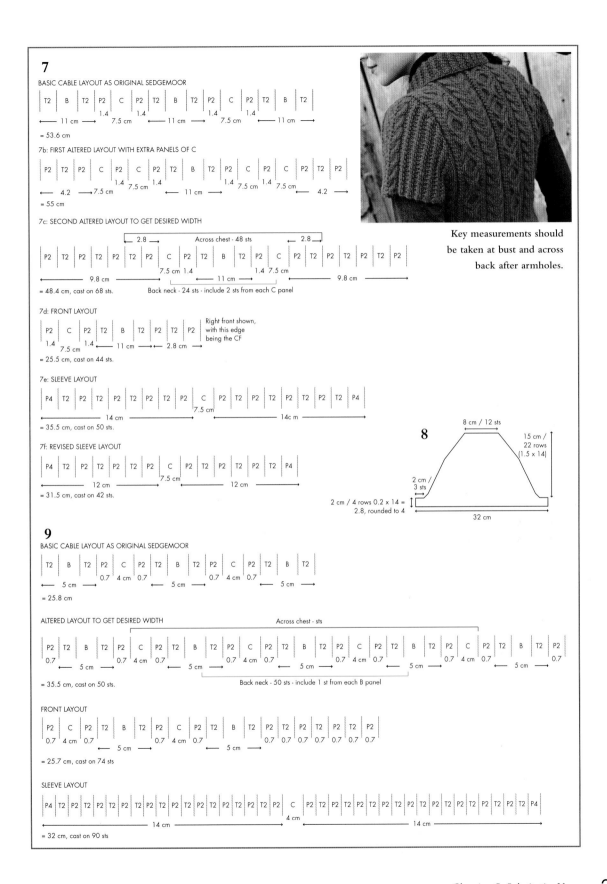

Key measurements should
be taken at bust and across
back after armholes.

8

8 cm / 12 sts

15 cm /
22 rows
(1.5 x 14)

2 cm /
3 sts

2 cm / 4 rows 0.2 x 14 =
2.8, rounded to 4

32 cm

9

BASIC CABLE LAYOUT AS ORIGINAL SEDGEMOOR

| T2 | B | T2 | P2 | C | P2 | T2 | B | T2 | P2 | C | P2 | T2 | B | T2 |

0.7   4 cm   0.7   0.7   4 cm   0.7

←— 5 cm —→   ←— 5 cm —→   ←— 5 cm —→

= 25.8 cm

ALTERED LAYOUT TO GET DESIRED WIDTH

Across chest - sts

| P2 | T2 | B | T2 | P2 | C | P2 | T2 | B | T2 | P2 | C | P2 | T2 | B | T2 | P2 | C | P2 | T2 | B | T2 | P2 |

0.7   4 cm   0.7   0.7   4 cm   0.7   0.7   4 cm   0.7   0.7   4 cm   0.7

←— 5 cm —→ ←— 5 cm —→ ←— 5 cm —→ ←— 5 cm —→ ←— 5 cm —→

= 35.5 cm, cast on 50 sts.

Back neck - 50 sts - include 1 st from each B panel

FRONT LAYOUT

| P2 | C | P2 | T2 | B | T2 | P2 | C | P2 | T2 | B | T2 | P2 | T2 | P2 | T2 | P2 |

0.7 4 cm 0.7   0.7 4 cm 0.7   0.7 0.7 0.7 0.7 0.7 0.7

←— 5 cm —→   ←— 5 cm —→

= 25.7 cm, cast on 74 sts.

SLEEVE LAYOUT

| P4 | T2 | P2 | T2 | P2 | T2 | P2 | T2 | P2 | T2 | P2 | T2 | P2 | T2 | P2 | C | P2 | T2 | P2 | T2 | P2 | T2 | P2 | T2 | P2 | T2 | P2 | T2 | P2 | P4 |

4 cm

←————— 14 cm —————→   ←————— 14 cm —————→

= 32 cm, cast on 90 sts

SEDGEMOOR CARDIGAN
Amanda Crawford

**Exquisite diamond-effect and twisted cables make this
texture-filled cardigan an interesting knit.**

Great for layering, this stylish cardigan design,
created by Amanda Crawford, is sure to become a
fashion staple of your winter wardrobe.

Amanda explains, 'I was inspired by a
waistcoat design that I'd seen on a catwalk model,
and thought a cabled, shaped cardigan would be
great as a hand knit.' Wear it layered over another
top as we have shown here, or with a belt, or
even in an evening outfit worn either fastened or
open to complement a pretty dress.

Amanda chose Debbie Bliss' Fez yarn, which
introduces us to the wonderfully soft properties
of camel hair. Fez is 15% camel and 85% extra
fine merino wool.

Fez is a superb blend – very smooth to knit
with and particularly well suited to textural designs.
Amanda says, 'It is so soft and really makes all the
cables and stitch interest stand out really well.

'I actually decided to knit Sedgemoor on
smaller needles than those suggested on the ball
band, as I think it helps to keep the fabric more
stable and make those cables really tight!'

SIZE

	8	10	12	14	16	18	20	22	
To Fit	81	86	91	96	101	107	112	117	cm
Bust	32	34	36	38	40	42	44	46	in
Actual	81	86	91	96	101	107	112	117	cm
Size	32	34	36	38	40	42	44	46	in
Actual	50	50	51	51	52	52	53	53	cm
Length	19½	19½	20	20	20½	20½	21	21	in

YARN

Debbie Bliss Fez (85% extra fine merino wool, 15% camel; 100m/50g balls)

Shade	8	8	9	9	10	11	11	12	x 50g
08									balls

NEEDLES & ACCESSORIES

1 pair 4.5mm (UK 7/US 7) knitting needles
Cable needle (cn), 3 x 20mm buttons

TENSION

26 sts and 28 rows to 10cm over pattern using 4.5mm needles

SPECIAL ABBREVIATIONS

T2: Twist 2 by taking right-hand needle to back of work and knitting into the back of second st on left-hand needle, then knit into back of first st and slip both sts together

C4F: Slip next 2 sts to cn and hold at front of work, K2, then K2 from cn

C4B: Slip next 2 sts to cn and hold at back of work, K2, then K2 from cn

C4FP: Slip next 2 sts to cn and hold at front of work, K2, then P2 from cn

C4BP: Slip next 2 sts to cn and hold at back of work, P2, then K2 from cn

T4F: Slip next 2 sts to cn and hold at front of work, P2, then K2 from cn

T4B: Slip next 2 sts to cn and hold at back of work, K2, then P2 from cn

Back

Using 4.5mm needles cast on 106 (112: 118: 124: 132: 140: 146: 150) sts.

Row 1 (RS): P3 (2: 1: 4: 4: 4: 3: 1), (T2, P2) 4 (5: 6: 6: 7: 8: 9: 10) times, ★Chart A row 1, (P2, T2) 5 times, P2; rep from ★ 1 more time, Chart A row 1, (P2, T2) 4 (5: 6: 6: 7: 8: 9: 10) times, P3 (2: 1: 4: 4: 4: 3: 1).

Row 2 (WS): K3 (2: 1: 4: 4: 4: 3: 1), (P2, K2) 4 (5: 6: 6: 7: 8: 9: 10) times, ★Chart A row 2, (K2, P2) 5 times, K2; rep from ★ once more, Chart A row 1, (K2, P2) 4 (5: 6: 6: 7: 8: 9: 10) times, K3 (2: 1: 4: 4: 4: 3: 1).

These 2 rows set the pattern for the lower border.

Continue to work, using appropriate row of Chart A, until 30 rows have been worked in total, ending with a WS row using row 6 of Chart A.

Next row: P3 (2: 1: 4: 4: 4: 3: 1), (T2, P2) 4 (5: 6: 6: 7: 8: 9: 10) times, ★C4F, C4B, (P2, T2) 5 times, P2; rep from ★ once more, C4F, C4B, (P2, T2) 4 (5: 6: 6: 7: 8: 9: 10) times, P3 (2: 1: 4: 4: 4: 3: 1).

Next row: K3 (2: 1: 4: 4: 4: 3: 1), (P2, K2) 4 (5: 6: 6: 7: 8: 9: 10) times, ★P8, (K2, P2) 5 times, K2; rep from ★ 1 more time, P8, (K2, P2) 4 (5: 6: 6: 7: 8: 9: 10) times, K3 (2: 1: 4: 4: 4: 3: 1).

Border pattern is now complete. Main body cable pattern placement is set by the following row:

Row 1 (RS): P3 (2: 1: 4: 4: 4: 3: 1), (T2, P2) 0 (1: 2: 2: 3: 4: 5: 6) times, ★Chart C row 1, P2, T2, Chart B row 1, T2, P2; rep from ★ to last 13 (16: 19: 22: 26: 30: 33: 35) sts, Chart C row 1, (P2, T2) 0 (1: 2: 2: 3: 4: 5: 6) times, P3 (2: 1: 4: 4: 4: 3: 1).

Row 2: K3 (2: 1: 4: 4: 4: 3: 1), (P2, K2) 0 (1: 2: 2: 3: 4: 5: 6) times, ★Chart C row 2, K2, P2, Chart B row 2, P2, K2; rep from ★ twice more, Chart C row 2, (K2, P2) 0 (1: 2: 2: 3: 4: 5: 6) times, K3 (2: 1: 4: 4: 4: 3: 1).

Cont in patt as set by last 2 rows, repeating charts as necessary, until work meas 30cm, ending RS facing for next row.

Armholes

Keeping patt correct cast off 5 (5: 5: 5: 6: 6: 6: 6) sts at beg of next 2 rows. 96 (102: 108: 114: 120: 128: 134: 138) sts.

Dec 1 st each end of next 3 rows then every foll alt row to 78 (80: 86: 90: 96: 102: 106: 112) sts.

Keeping patt correct cont in patt until armhole meas 19 (19: 20: 20: 21: 21: 22: 22) cm ending with RS facing for next row.

Shoulders

Cast off 8 (9: 10: 11: 12: 13: 13: 15) sts at beg of next 2 rows then 8 (8: 10: 11: 11: 13: 13: 14) sts at beg of foll 2 rows.

Cast off rem 46 (46: 46: 46: 50: 50: 54: 54) sts.

Left front

Using 4.5mm needles cast on 57 (60: 63: 66: 70: 74: 77: 79) sts.

Row 1 (RS): P3 (2: 1: 4: 4: 4: 3: 1), (T2, P2) 4 (5: 6: 6: 7: 8: 9: 10) times, Chart A row 1, (P2, T2) 7 times, P2.

Row 2: K2, (P2, K2) 7 times, Chart A row 2, (K2, P2) 4 (5: 6: 6: 7: 8: 9: 10) times, K3 (2: 1: 4: 4: 4: 3: 1).

These 2 rows set the pattern for the lower border.

Continue to work, using appropriate row of Chart A, until 30 rows have been worked in total, ending with a WS row using row 6 of Chart A.

Next row: P3 (2: 1: 4: 4: 4: 3: 1), (T2, P2) 4 (5: 6: 6: 7: 8: 9: 10) times, C4F, C4B, (P2, T2) 7 times, P2.

Next row: K2, (P2, K2) 7 times, P8, (K2, P2) 4 (5: 6: 6: 7: 8: 9: 10) times, K3 (2: 1: 4: 4: 4: 3: 1).

Border pattern is now complete. Main body cable pattern placement is set by the following row:

Row 1 (RS): P3 (2: 1: 4: 4: 4: 3: 1), (T2, P2) 0 (1: 2: 2: 3: 4: 5: 6) times, Chart C row 1, P2, T2, Chart B row 1, T2, P2,

Chart C row 1, P2, (T2, P2) 3 times.
Row 2: (K2, P2) 3 times, K2, Chart C row 2, K2, P2, Chart B row 2, P2, K2, Chart C row 2, (K2, P2) 0 (1: 2: 2: 3: 4: 5: 6) times, K3 (2: 1: 4: 4: 4: 3: 1).
Cont in patt as set by last 2 rows following charts until work meas same as Back to beg of armhole shaping, ending with RS facing for next row.

Armhole and neck edge

Keeping patt correct cast off 5 (5: 5: 5: 6: 6: 6: 6) sts at beg of next row, patt to last 4 sts, K2tog, P2. 51 (54: 57: 60: 63: 67: 70: 72) sts.
Cont to dec 1 st at armhole edge of next 3 rows then foll 6 (8: 8: 9: 9: 10: 11: 10) alt rows AT SAME TIME cont to dec 1 st at neck edge, 2 sts in, on next 8 rows then every alt row until 16 (17: 20: 22: 23: 26: 26: 29) sts rem.
Keeping patt correct cont in patt until armhole meas same as Back to beg of shoulder shaping ending with RS facing for next row.

Shoulder

Cast off 8 (9: 10: 11: 12: 13: 13: 15) sts at beg of next row.
Work 1 row straight.
Cast off rem 8 (8: 10: 11: 11: 13: 13: 14) sts.
Mark positions for 3 buttons on edge of Left Front. The first button to sit at top of border and the third to sit just below start of neck shaping and the second to be in the middle of these 2.

Right front

Using 4.5mm needles cast on 57 (60: 63: 66: 70: 74: 77: 79) sts.
Row 1 (RS): (P2, T2) 7 times, P2, Chart A row 1, (P2, T2) 4 (5: 6: 6: 7: 8: 9: 10) times, P3 (2: 1: 4: 4: 4: 3: 1).
Row 2: K3 (2: 1: 4: 4: 4: 3: 1), (P2, K2) 4 (5: 6: 6: 7: 8: 9: 10) times, Chart A row 1, (K2, P2) 7 times, K2.
These 2 rows set the pattern for the lower border.
Continue to work, using appropriate row of Chart A, until 30 rows have been worked in total, ending with a WS row using row 6 of Chart A.
Next row: (P2, T2) 7 times, P2, C4F, C4B, (P2, T2) 4 (5: 6: 6: 7: 8: 9: 10) times, P3 (2: 1: 4: 4: 4: 3: 1).
Next row: K3 (2: 1: 4: 4: 4: 3: 1), (P2, K2) 4 (5: 6: 6: 7: 8: 9: 10) times, P8, (K2, P2) 7 times, K2.
Border pattern is now complete. Main body cable pattern placement is set by the following row:
Row 1 (RS): P2, (T2, P2) 3 times, Chart C row 1, P2, T2, Chart B row 1, T2, P2, Chart C row 1, (P2, T2) 0 (1: 2: 2: 3: 4: 5: 6) times, P3 (2: 1: 4: 4: 4: 3: 1).
Row 2: K3 (2: 1: 4: 4: 4: 3: 1), (P2, K2) 0 (1: 2: 2: 3: 4: 5: 6) times, Chart C row 2, K2, P2, Chart B row 2, P2, K2, Chart C row 2, (K2, P2) 3 times, K2.
Make your first buttonhole on next RS row, 6 sts in from edge, over 3 sts by casting off 3 sts and casting on 3 sts over 3 cast off sts on foll row.
Complete to match Left Front reversing shapings and working patt as set by last row following charts placing buttonholes to correspond with markers for buttons.

Sleeves

Using 4.5mm needles cast on 88 (88: 94: 94: 100: 100: 106: 106) sts.
Row 1 (RS): P3 (3: 2: 2: 1: 1: 4: 4), (T2, P2) 9 (9: 10: 10: 11: 11: 11: 11) times, Chart C row 1, (P2, T2) 9 (9: 10: 10: 11: 11: 11: 11) times, P3 (3: 2: 2: 1: 1: 4: 4).
Row 2: K3 (3: 2: 2: 1: 1: 4: 4), (P2, K2) 9 (9: 10: 10: 11: 11:

11: 11) times, Chart C row 2, (K2, P2) 9 (9: 10: 10: 11: 11: 11: 11) times, K3 (3: 2: 2: 1: 1: 4: 4).

These 2 rows set position of patt. Cont in patt for 4 rows in total ending with RS facing for next row.

Sleevehead

Keeping patt correct cast off 5 (5: 5: 5: 6: 6: 6: 6) sts at beg of next 2 rows. 78 (78: 84: 84: 88: 88: 94: 94) sts.

Dec 1 st each end of next 3 rows then every foll alt row to 46 (46: 56: 56: 58: 58: 64: 64) sts and every row until 26 sts rem.

Cast off.

Making up

Press carefully following instructions on ball band.
Join shoulder seams.

Collar

Using 4.5mm needles with WS facing pick up and K54 (54: 56: 56: 60: 60: 62: 62) sts up left front neck edge, 46 (46: 46: 46: 50: 50: 50: 50) sts across back neck and 54 (54: 56: 56: 60: 60: 62: 62) sts down right front. 154 (154: 158: 158: 170: 170: 174: 174) sts.

Row 1 (WS): K2, ★P2, K2; rep from ★ to end.
Row 2 (RS): P2, ★T2, P2; rep from ★ to end.
These 2 rows form twisted rib.

Next row: As row 1.
Next row: P2, T2, P2tog, patt to last 6 sts, P2tog, T2, P2.
Cont to dec each end of every row 4 sts in from edge, until 102 (102: 106: 106: 118: 118: 122: 122) sts rem.
Next row (WS): K2, P2, (K2tog, P2) 5 (5: 5: 5: 7: 7: 7: 7) times, patt 54 (54: 58: 58: 54: 54: 58: 58) sts, (P2, K2tog) 5 (5: 5: 5: 7: 7: 7: 7) times, P2, K2.
92 (92: 96: 96: 104: 104: 108: 108) sts.
Cast off in rib.
Set in sleeves and join side and underarm seams. Weave in all ends.

In detail

If you have never tried cabling without using a cable needle, Sedgemoor would be a fantastic project to try out this speedy technique. C4F: Slip 2 sts purlwise, then K2. Slide your LH needle into the front of the 2 slipped sts, pinch the knitting below all 4 sts and remove the RH needle from all 4 sts. The LH needle is holding 2 sts, so just pick up the 2 sts that are hanging loose, with your LH needle. You have now twisted the sts, so just K2 to finish. See Masterclass 4 for more detailed explanation.

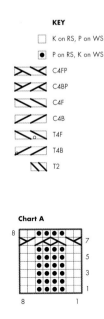

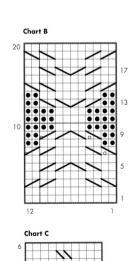

KEY

☐	K on RS, P on WS
⬛	P on RS, K on WS
✕	C4FP
✕	C4BP
╲	C4F
╱	C4B
╲	T4F
╱	T4B
⤺	T2

2 CASTING ON & CASTING OFF

Casting on is, by necessity, the foundation of our knitting and, together with casting off, is a technique we may barely think about. Our choice of technique can have a dramatic effect on the finished look of our projects. There are many ways to cast on and cast off, so we have selected three methods that will help you to finesse your knitting to the next level.

TUBULAR CAST ON & CAST OFF
Jane Crowfoot

Have you ever noticed how the bottom and top edges (that is, the cast-on edge and the cast-off edge) of machine-knitted fabrics vary from those created by hand knitting?

Go and grab a machine-knit sweater and take a look – so long as the sweater you have chosen has not been cut and then sewn together using an overlocker, you will see that the welts do not have a clear edge and that the stitches do not appear to manifest from a line of cast on stitches. This is referred to as 'tubular' or 'invisible' cast on and cast off and is relatively easy for a hand knitter to achieve. It is ideal for 1x1 and 2x2 ribbing.

Another advantage of the tubular cast on, other than its 'invisible' nature, is its stretch. The tubular cast on is fantastic for top-down socks, while its cast off equivalent is perfect for toe-up socks. So follow this easy guide to get to grips with tidy edges in no time.

Tubular cast on

This method creates a firm edge as your tube rows only use half of the total number of stitches. The following method creates single rib.

You will need enough waste yarn to work at least 5 rows. Choose yarn of the same ply as your main yarn and, if possible, pick a strongly contrasting colour.

Using the waste yarn, cast on half the number of stitches required by the main piece of knitting. See further details below. Work a few rows in stocking stitch, ending with a WS row – 4 rows should be enough.

1   Join in the main yarn and work 4 rows in stocking stitch ending with RS facing. (When joining in the new yarn do not weave in the yarn end.)

2   You will be picking up stitches along the row where the colours changed so take a moment to make sure you understand into which stitches you will be working. With the wrong side of the work facing, you should be able to clearly see the colour change row. You will see that there is a row of loops in the main colour sitting between rows in the contrast colour. It is the line of stitches in the main colour that you need to pick up.

3   Knit the first stitch.

4   ★ Use the right needle to pick up the first loop that you can see in the main colour along the row where you changed colour.

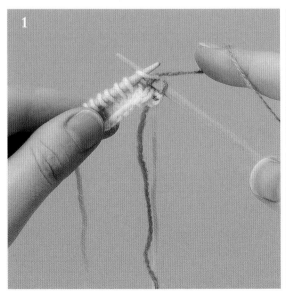

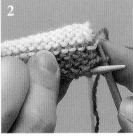

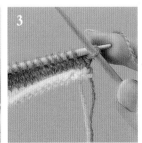

5 Place the yarn loop on the left needle.

6 Bring the yarn to the front, then purl the stitch onto the right needle.

7 Take the yarn back and knit the next stitch from the LH needle.

8 Repeat from ★ to the end of the row.

If the final stitch of the row is to be a purl stitch you may find it difficult to identify it, but so long as you pick up a loop of yarn in the correct colour along the correct row you cannot go too far wrong.

9+10 When the row is complete you can carefully remove the waste yarn. Be careful and make sure that you cut the correct yarn away. To be totally sure of not making a mess, it is a good idea to unravel stitch by stitch.

This method can also be used just as successfully starting work with the main yarn on a WS row, and working the picking up loops row on a WS row as well. In this case, you purl the sts already on the needle and take yarn to back before knitting the picked up loops.

TIP: To get an even more stretchy edge, you may want to work the first 4 rows in the main colour using a size larger needle than is required.

This method can also be used for stocking stitch, but it will not create an invisible edge; however, it will prevent your knitting from curling if you want to go straight into stocking stitch.

How many stitches to cast on?

When you look at the WS of the row where main yarn and waste yarn meet, you will see that there is one less loop to pick up than stitches cast on. So if you cast on 10 stitches, you will see 9 main yarn loops. If you require an odd number of stitches, divide the total number that you need by two and round up to a whole number. So if you need 29 sts of ribbing: $29 \div 2 = 14.5$. This rounds up to 15 sts. So you cast on 15 sts and pick up 14 loops, thus making 29 stitches in total.

If you need an even number of stitches there are two options. Either you can cast on half of the required number and work a single increase at the end of the pick-up row, or you can cast on one more than half the number of stitches, and work a single decrease at the end of the pick-up row.

2x2 ribbing

You can also use the tubular method to start 2x2 rib, by simply knitting the first 2 stitches and then picking up 2 loops from the first main yarn row. Repeat this, alternating to the end of the row.

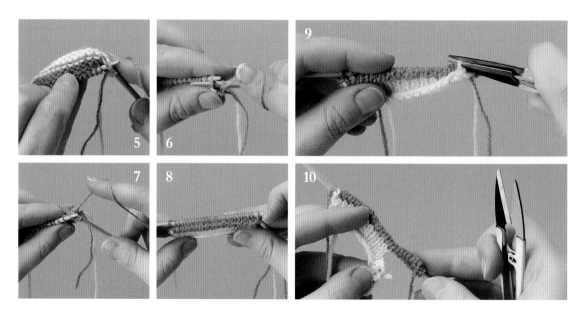

Tubular cast off

You can create a cast-off edge that matches the cast on perfectly, by using the tubular method.

11 Work your ribbing as normal until you are 2 rows short of the desired length.

12 Work 4 rows slipping all of the purl sts with the yarn in front, and knitting all of the knit stitches.

13 Slip alternate stitches onto two double-pointed or circular needles, thus dividing the stitches into two layers. The knit stitches should be on the row closest to you, and the purls behind.

14 Graft the two layers of stitches together using Kitchener stitch as follows:

Set up: Thread a tapestry needle with a long length of yarn and pass it through the first stitch on the needle closest to you as if to purl.

Pass it through the first stitch on the rear needle as if to knit. Pull gently to tighten, but not over-tighten, the yarn. It is easy to tighten it later.

Grafting: ★ Pass the needle through the first stitch on the front needle as if to knit and slip it off the needle. Pass it through the next stitch on the front needle as if to purl, but don't slip it off.

Pass the needle through the first stitch on the rear needle as if to purl and slip it off the needle. Pass it through the next stitch on the rear needle as if to knit, but don't slip it off.

Rep from ★ until all stitches are joined.

You can then work along the row carefully neatening and tightening up the stitches.

We find the following rhyme helps us to remember the process:

Knit slip, purl. Purl slip, knit.

Then all you need to remember is the set up, which is the second part of each half of the phrase (purl, then knit).

If your cast-off edge seems a little looser than the cast on, it may be because you have knitted more loosely in the rows where you are slipping alternate stitches. If this is a problem, then you can simply work these rows with a size smaller needle.

As for the cast on, this method can also be used for 2x2 ribbing; simply follow the instructions, but slip alternate pairs of sts onto two DPNs to separate the layers.

PROVISIONAL CAST ON METHODS
Jane Crowfoot

Like many knitters, you may be of the opinion that life is too short to learn more than one cast on method. Rest assured that using the correct cast on for your project really can make a difference to the finished outcome, so it's worth investigating what's appropriate for the type of project you're knitting. Indeed, some cast ons create sturdy, obvious edges, whilst others can be very elastic or virtually invisible.

In the case of lace knitting, it is more important than ever to consider carefully which cast on you are going to use. This decision is less vital when knitting a garment as the pieces will require some straight edges (as at shoulders for example). However, if you are choosing to knit a lace shawl or throw you may want each end of the piece to appear the same. This is especially the case if working a piece that creates a zig-zag, chevron or peaked edge.

Different cast on methods

There are many cast ons suitable for lace and you will find an abundance of them on the internet. They are often referred to as 'invisible' or 'provisional' cast ons and many techniques have no definitive, dedicated name. Take time to decide which cast on you need to use, and if the designer has suggested a particular method, then our advice is to use it because they have usually specified it for a reason!

The key to a good cast on is even tension that allows you to work the first row with ease. If you find that your cast on is too tight, then you could decide to use a size larger knitting needle for the cast on only.

1+2 To demonstrate the differences, we have knitted and blocked these two swatches. The first has been worked with a provisional cast on this was then removed and a small knitted-on garter stitch border worked to cast off the live stitches at top and bottom. The second swatch was started using a lace (or knitted) cast on, and finished with a K2tog cast off. It was very difficult to block the second swatch evenly, hence the trapezium-shaped finish, due to the differing tightness of the cast on and cast-off edges. In comparison, the first swatch blocked not only evenly, but more fully, due to the greater stretch of knitted fabric.

If you want a smooth straight edge, a standard cast on may be more suitable, as it gives a firm line. You will just need to choose your needle sizes carefully so that the edges match.

Lace patterns often use a range of techniques to avoid cast-on and cast-off edges. Starting with a provisional or invisible cast on is just one of these techniques. Other techniques might include working from the centre outwards, knitting sideways borders onto live stitches, and grafting.

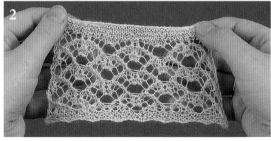

Invisible cast on using a crochet chain

How to make the foundation chain

These stitches form the basis of the work and are equivalent to a cast on in knitting.

You may find that you struggle to keep an even tension. It is important to keep the chains to the same tension and not to make them too tight or loose; with practice you should find that this becomes easier. Always use a separate piece of waste yarn, preferably in a contrast colour, and make the chain longer than the required number of stitches so that you have plenty of 'normal' chain stitches and are not attempting to work into slip knots or really tight stitches. For safety, place the final chain on a stitch holder or safety pin.

Place a slip knot on the hook and hold it in the right hand. Hold the yarn in the left hand using your preferred method and at the same time keep a good tension on the tail end of the yarn. With the yarn sitting to the reverse of the hook, turn the hook so that it is facing away from you.

★ Push the crochet hook against the yarn then rotate the hook in a clockwise direction in order to catch the yarn around the hook, finishing the step with the hook facing down. Draw the yarn through the slip knot.

Continue to rotate the hook clockwise, so that the hook is left facing up and a new stitch is resting on the hook.

Continue to work from ★ to create more chain. You will need to reposition the tensioning fingers of your left hand every couple of stitches to ensure a good tension.

TIP: When making a chain (or subsequent stitches) you must make sure that each stitch is taken up onto the thicker part of the hook before starting the next one. If you work your stitches on the thinner part of the hook they will become tight and you will struggle to place your hook or needle into them on subsequent rows.

It is important that you can recognise the formation of each chain and thus count correctly.

1 The front of the chain looks like a series of V shapes made by the yarn. Each V sits in a chain between one above and one below. The surface of the chain is smooth on this side.

2 The reverse of the chain has a row of bumps which have been created by the yarn. These bumps sit behind the V and run in a vertical direction from the beginning of the chain up to the hook. The surface of the reverse of the chain is more textural than the front side.

3 Place your knitting needle through the required number of bumps on the back of the chain so that the chain sits like stitches on your knitting needle.

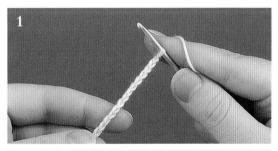

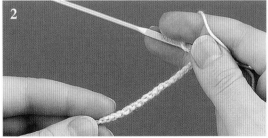

Unravelling the waste yarn

Work from your pattern until you need to work away from the cast on in the opposite direction.

Being REALLY careful, unravel the crochet chain by pulling on gently on the waste yarn. This will leave you with open (or 'live') stitches.

As you unravel each chain, place the live stitch onto your knitting needle, being careful not to twist the stitches.

Continue from pattern, but see Note about number of stitches on page 35.

Knitting with waste yarn

This is a nifty way of working and is ultra safe too as stitches are unlikely to unravel. The only scary bit is cutting the yarn when you need to return to the second piece of knitting, so just take your time to ensure that you are cutting the right piece. To make this easier you may want to use a cotton yarn as this will not mat or felt together with the chosen garment yarn. Also it is a good idea to use a waste yarn that is the same weight as the garment yarn; this will mean that the open stitches achieve the correct tension.

Using a piece of waste yarn, cast on using your preferred method – such as cable or thumb method – and work a few rows in stocking stitch.

1   Swap to your project yarn (shown here in green) and work in pattern. Once you have completed this first piece snip one end of the waste yarn on the last row of stocking stitch.

Being REALLY careful, unravel the row of stocking stitch until the waste piece of stocking stitch has fallen away. This will leave you with open (or 'live') stitches.

2   As you unravel each stitch, place the live stitch onto your knitting needle, being careful not to twist the stitches.

Continue from pattern, but see Note about number of stitches on page 35.

Yarn over needle invisible cast on

1 Place a slip knot on your knitting needle. Hold the needle in your right hand, holding the tail end of the working yarn and one end of the waste yarn out of the way. Hold the yarns with your left hand, with the waste yarn nearer you and over your thumb, and the 'garment' yarn over your index finger.

2 ⋆ Place the knitting needle under the waste yarn.

3 Catch the garment yarn using your knitting needle, then bring it under the waste yarn to the front in order to create a stitch on the needle.

4 From above the waste yarn, pick up the garment yarn and bring the needle back towards you to make another stitch.

Repeat from ⋆ until you have the correct number of stitches. You will find that you need to push the stitches down the needle in small groups as you make your stitches. Try to spread them out evenly; this will help you achieve an even tension.

5 The cast on is created by wrapping the yarn around both the knitting needle and the waste yarn. Every stitch on one part of the needle has a corresponding stitch on the waste yarn, so it is probably best that you think of the stitches as pairs. You will see that you have one predominant stitch and one smaller one sitting below it on the waste yarn – this is a pair.

When you need to pick up the stitches from the cast-on row, transfer the stitches on the waste yarn, one by one, to a spare needle being careful not to twist them and undo the slip knot at the beginning of the row.

Continue from pattern, but see Note below about number of stitches.

Note

Once you have unravelled the provisional cast on and are thus working with stitches that do not have a defined cast on edge, you will notice that when picking up the unravelled stitches in order to recommence your piece, you will have one stitch fewer than the required stitch count. (This is because of the way knitted stitches are made.) To rectify this, you can either cast on one extra stitch at the beginning of the first piece of knitting, or you can make a stitch at some point through the first row of the second piece.

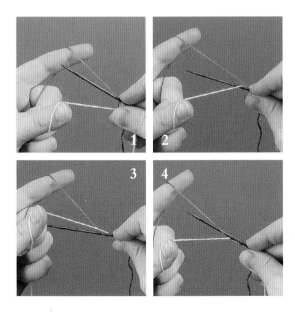

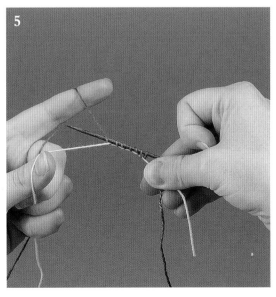

JUDY BECKER'S MAGIC CAST ON
Judy Becker

There are many advantages to knitting socks from the toe upwards. For example, the sock can be tried on as you go, so the fit is perfect. If you are not sure you have enough yarn, you can knit both socks at the same time and stop when your yarn runs out.

Frustrated that none of the methods she tried were ideal, Judy Becker developed her own 'Magic Cast On'. It's an easy-to-learn, fast method that works the first time, every time. It's completely invisible from both sides, and it can be used with almost any pattern that calls for a provisional cast on - including, of course, socks.

These instructions assume that you have some familiarity with knitting socks toe-up. The photos show circular needles, but you can also use DPNs.

A note about stitch mount: Whether the leading leg of a stitch is in front of or behind the needle is determined by the direction you wrap the yarn around the needles. If you wrap the yarn as shown in the photos, the leading leg will be in front of the needle. But wrapping in either direction will work fine - wrap in the direction that is comfortable for you. If one or more stitches are mounted with the leading leg behind the needle, knit each of these stitches through the middle so they are not twisted.

Casting on

1   Hold a needle parallel to the floor with the tip pointing to your left. Loop the yarn around the needle with the tail towards the front and the working yarn (the strand attached to the skein) towards the back.

2   With your left hand, pick up the yarn so that the tail goes over your index finger and the working yarn goes over your thumb. This will make a loop around the top needle that counts as the first stitch.

3   Place a second needle underneath the first needle with the tip pointing to the left. The bottom needle will be loaded with stitches from the tail yarn that's over your finger. The top needle will be loaded with stitches from the working yarn over your thumb.

4   While holding the loop in place with a finger on your right hand, bring the tip of the bottom needle over the strand of yarn on your finger. Loop the yarn around and over the bottom needle and down between both needles. Return the needles to their starting position.

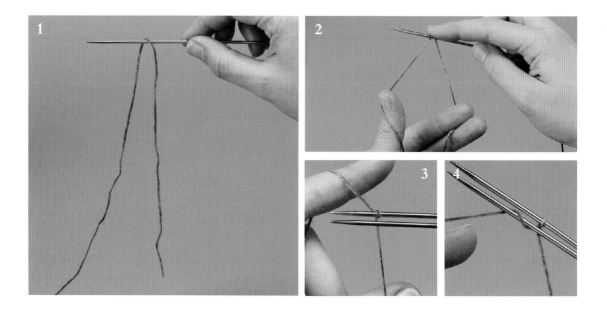

Pull the loop snug, but not tight, around the needle. Try for your usual knitting tension. You have cast 1 stitch onto the bottom needle.

5   Bring the top needle over the yarn tail on your thumb. Loop the yarn between the needles, around and over the top needle, and back behind the needle. Return the needles to their starting position. Pull the loop snug around the needle, trying for your usual knitting tension.

You have cast 1 stitch onto the top needle. There are now 2 stitches on the top needle: the stitch you just cast on, plus the first loop.

Repeat step 4 to cast a second stitch onto the bottom needle. Repeat step 5 to cast a third stitch onto the top needle.

Continue repeating steps 4 and 5 until you have cast on the desired number of stitches. You should have the same number of stitches on each needle.

6   In this picture, a total of 20 stitches, or 10 stitches on each needle, have been cast on. The side facing you looks like 2 rows of offset loops.

7   If you turn the needles over, you will see that the other side of the work (which will become the inside of your sock) features a row of purl bumps between the needles.

Knitting the first round

Rnd 1, First Side: Drop the yarn tail and let it dangle. Turn the needles so that the tips point to the right, both needles are parallel to the floor, and the purl bump side is up. You will knit from the needle closest to you. Pull the needle furthest away from you to the right until the stitches lie on the cable. Pick up the working yarn.

8   Be sure that the yarn tail lies between the working yarn and the needle. In the picture, you can see how the tail passes under the working strand. You can hold the tail in your left hand for the first stitch or two to keep it stable.

9   Knit the row of stitches from the needle closest to you. Remember to knit all stitches through the middle to prevent twisted stitches. If the first stitch becomes loose, you can snug it up again by pulling gently on the tail. You will see a row of stitches appear between the two needles.

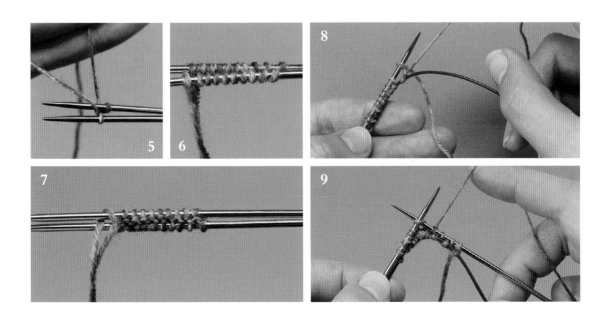

Rnd 1, Second Side: Turn the needles so that the tips point to the right, both needles are parallel to the floor and the purl bump side is up. Pull the needle furthest from you to the right so that the stitches you just knitted lie along the cable. Push the needle closest to you towards the left so the stitches are on the needle ready to knit.

10 Knit the stitches from the needle closest to you (knitting all stitches through the middle to prevent twisted stitches).

You have completed 1 round and are back where you started. There are 2 rows of stitches between the needles now. The absolute centre of your sock toe lies between the 2 rows of stitches.

Knitting a sock toe

The following instructions are for a typical toe-up sock that starts at the very end:

Rnd 2: On first needle, ★ K1, M1, K each st to within 1 stitch of the end of row, M1, K1, turn to second needle. Repeat from ★.
Rnd 3: K all stitches on both needles (no increases). Repeat these two rounds, increasing 4 stitches every other round, until you reach the desired number of stitches.

11 In this picture, 14 rounds have been worked and there are 28 stitches on each needle (56 stitches total).

12 Here you can see the toe spread out. The very end of the toe where the cast on was made is in the centre. You can see the stitches flow over the centre of the toe with no visible seam. The tail can be woven in and trimmed at any time after you've worked at least one non-increase round.

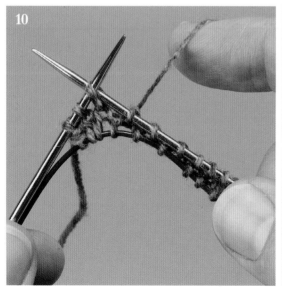

13 For two-at-a-time socks, drop both the tail and the working strands when you have cast on all the stitches for the first sock. Push the stitches back along the needles to make room for another set of stitches. Starting from a new ball of yarn or the other end of the first ball, cast a second set of stitches onto the same needles.

Rnd 1, First Side: Pick up the working yarn belonging to the stitches closest to the end of the needles. Knit the first set of stitches.

14 Drop the yarn and pick up the working yarn belonging to the next set of stitches. Knit the next set of stitches.

Rnd 2, Second Side: Pick up the working yarn of the stitches closest to the end of the needles. Knit the first set of stitches. Drop the yarn and pick up the working yarn belonging to the next set of stitches. Knit the next set of stitches.

Working with DPNs

If you are knitting with double-pointed needles (DPNs), cast onto two needles.

15 Work Rnd 1, First Side by knitting half of the stitches using one needle and the remaining half of the stitches using a second needle. Work Rnd 1, Second Side by knitting half the stitches using a third needle, and the remaining half the stitches using a fourth needle.

Non-sock projects

To start an oblong bag or purse, cast on enough stitches to equal the width of the bag minus the depth. Work round 1, then increase 4 stitches every round at 'corner' points until the bottom of the bag is the right size.

When casting on a centre-out project that begins with a small circle, cast on 4 to 6 total stitches. On the first round, hold the tail and working yarn together and knit with both, making two loops in each stitch. On the second round, knit each of those loops individually, doubling the number of stitches.

To use as a provisional cast on, starting a project in the middle and then knitting in both directions, cast the total number of stitches specified by the pattern onto each needle. This will be, counting both needles, double the cast on stitches called for by the pattern. Work the first row of the pattern across the first needle. Turn and work the second row of the pattern back along the same needle. When you complete the first half of the project, the remaining stitches cast onto the other needle will be ready to begin knitting the second half of the project.

And when anyone asks you how you accomplished that wonderful, invisible cast on, you can say, 'It's magic!'

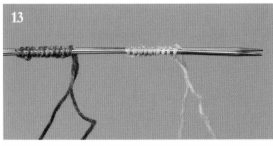

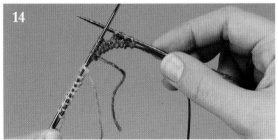

ELWOOD HAT
Kirstie McLeod

Rustle up this quick-knit hat with lace and cable patterning, using 4ply yarn from your stash.

Do you have odd balls of yarn in your stash crying out for a project to put them to use? Well, try this hat design using a chevron lace stitch pattern, interspersed with cabling. It uses the tubular cast on method, which is lovely and stretchy for a comfy fit.

Kirstie McLeod is the creator of this hat; she tells us: 'I really wanted to come up with a cosy hat design, that's interesting to knit but also that would be fairly speedy! I had some Jamieson and Smith Jumper Weight yarn left over from another project, so I figured this would be just a perfect way to use it up.

'Now I can't wait to try it in some other 4ply yarns – I think it makes a great gift knit, especially as it's the sort of relaxed shape that suits so many people.'

SIZE
Head diameter up to 54cm (21¼in)

YARN
Jamieson & Smith 2ply Jumper Weight (knits as 4ply; 100% Shetland wool; 115m/25g balls)
Shade FC15 3 x 25g balls

NEEDLES & ACCESSORIES
1 set 3.75mm (UK 9/US 5) circular needles, 40cm long, or set of four double-pointed needles in same size
Cable needle (cn), waste yarn

TENSION
28 sts and 40 rows to 10cm over cable and lace pattern using 3.75mm needles

SPECIAL ABBREVIATIONS
C6F: Sl 3 sts on to cn and hold at front, K3 and then K3 from cn

YARN SUBSTITUTION SUGGESTIONS
When substituting a yarn, remember that you need to use something that will knit to the same tension, and you will need the same total length of yarn for the pattern. For this hat, you will need approx 300m of 4ply yarn.

OTHER YARNS THAT YOU MAY LIKE TO TRY INCLUDE:
Fyberspates Sheila's Sock (100% superwash merino; 365m/100g skeins)
1 skein
Debbie Bliss Rialto 4ply (100% extrafine merino; 180m/50g balls)
2 balls
Artesano Alpaca 4ply (100% pure superfine alpaca; 184m/50g balls)
2 balls
Stylecraft Life 4ply (75% acrylic, 25% wool; 450m/100g balls)
1 ball

Lace and cable pattern

Worked over 21 sts and 8 rows.
Rnd 1: P3, K6, P3, yo, Sl 1, K1, psso, K5, K2tog, yo.
Rnd 2 and all even rounds: P3, K6, P3, K9.
Rnd 3: P3, K6, P3, K1, yo, Sl 1, K1, psso, K3, K2tog, yo, K1.
Rnd 5: P3, K6, P3, K2, yo, Sl 1, K1, psso, K1, K2tog, yo, K2.
Rnd 7: P3, C6F, P3, K3, yo, Sl 1, K2tog, psso, yo, K3.
Rnd 8: P3, K6, P3, K9.

Hat

Using 3.75mm circular needles or DPNs and waste yarn work a tubular cast on as follows:
Cast on 73 sts. Join to work in the round and work 5 rounds in st st.
Change to the main yarn, and work 4 more rounds in st st.
Next rnd: ★K1, yf, pick up the loop of main yarn, from the first row, between the 2 waste yarn sts and purl it, yb; rep from ★ to the end of the round. 146 sts.
Next rnd: ★K1, P1; rep from ★ to end. Continue working a 1x1 rib as set above for 9 further rounds, inc 1 st at end of last round. 147 sts.
Remove waste yarn from cast-on edge.
Start to work lace and cable pattern, repeating motif 7 times each round. Continue until 96 rounds have been worked in pattern (12 repeats).
Rnd 1: ★P2tog, P1, K6, P3, yo, Sl 1, K1, psso, K5, K2tog, yo; rep from ★ to end of round. 140 sts.
Rnd 2: ★P2, K6, P3, K9; rep from ★ to end of round.
Rnd 3: ★P2, K6, P2tog, P1, K1, yo, Sl 1, K1, psso, K3, K2tog, yo, K1; rep from ★ to end of round. 133 sts.
Rnd 4: ★P2, K6, P2, K9; rep from ★ to end of round.
Rnd 5: ★P2tog, K6, P2, K2, yo, Sl 1, K1, psso, K1, K2tog, yo, K2; rep from ★ to end of round. 126 sts.
Rnd 6: ★P1, K6, P2, K9; rep from ★ to end of round.
Rnd 7: ★P1, C6F, P2tog, K3, yo, Sl 1, K2tog, psso, yo, K3; rep from ★ to end of round. 119 sts.
Rnd 8: ★P1, K1, Sl 1, K1, psso, K3, P1, K9; rep from ★ to end of round. 112 sts.
Rnd 9: ★P1, K2, K2tog, K1, P1, yo, Sl 1, K1, psso, K5, K2tog, yo; rep from ★ to end. 105 sts.
Rnd 10: ★P1, K4, P1, Sl 1, K1, psso, K5, K2tog; rep from ★ to end. 91 sts.
Rnd 11: ★P1, K4, P1, Sl 1, K1, psso, K3, K2tog; rep from ★ to end. 77 sts.
Rnd 12: ★P1, K4, P1, Sl 1, K1, psso, K1, K2tog; rep from ★ to end. 63 sts.
Rnd 13: ★P1, Sl 1, K1, psso, K2tog, P1, K3; rep from ★ to end. 49 sts.
Rnd 14: ★P1, K2, P1, Sl 1, K2tog, psso; rep from ★ to end. 35 sts.

Thread yarn through sts and secure. Weave in all loose ends. Hand wash and re-shape while wet.

3 DIFFERENT STYLES OF KNITTING

We love techniques that improve the basics of our knitting, whether it be an easier way to knit in the round or a technique that makes the simplest construction look perfect. If you love circular needles but don't know how to use them for small diameter knitting, then try the 'Magic Loop' technique. If your tension tends to be slack, try Combination knitting – you may well be amazed at the difference it makes.

SMALL DIAMETER KNITTING IN THE ROUND
Jane Crowfoot

If you are making socks, mittens and sleeves we have a couple of techniques to help you work with small diameter knitting in the round. You are going to love these methods, which will be sure to help (and impress) you.

It isn't unheard of for even the most accomplished of knitters to find knitting small pieces in the round tricky. If you have a small number of stitches on a circular needle then, regardless of how long the cable is or how short the actual needle part is, you'll be working at a tighter angle when inserting into the stitches.

Here we'll show you two great ways for working small diameter knitting. The first uses two circular needles to hold the stitches; the second is the 'Magic Loop' technique which uses just one circular needle. Both are easy, will prevent stretched, uneven stitches and will make your knitting process much easier.

Using two circular needles

At first, it is a good idea to use two differing sets of circular needles; whilst they obviously need to be the same diameter and it is logical (although not essential) to use needles with the same length wire, try to find needles either with different coloured points or points made from different materials, such as a metal pair and a wooden pair for example.

Cast the required number of stitches onto one of the circular needles (here shown in metal) using your preferred method.

1 Using the second set of circulars (shown here in wood), knit across half the number of stitches.

2 Hold both sets of needles in your left hand with the stitches you have already knitted on the back needle and both needles with the tips facing to the right.

3 ★ Pull the back needle through the stitches so that the stitches sit on the wire. Pick up the other end of the circular needle that you are holding to the front (shown here in metal) and knit across the stitches on this needle.

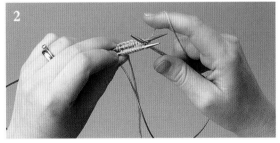

4 Transfer both needles to your left hand once again, this time with the wooden needles at the front. Slip the stitches just worked onto the cable and slide the stitches on the wooden needle onto the tip pointing right. Use the other end of the wooden needles to knit across these stitches.

5 Continue to repeat from *, turning the work after each set of stitches and ensuring that you always work stitches onto the tip of the same needle. So if the stitches start on the wooden needles, you need to knit them onto the other end of the wooden needles.

3 Turn the work so that the tips of the needles are pointing to the right, and slide the stitches on the front half so that they are sitting on the tip of the needle, leaving the stitches behind on the wire. Make sure that the stitches are not twisted.

4 * Pick up the other end of the circular needle and knit across the stitches from the front needle tip. Transfer both needle tips to your left hand once again (the needle with the stitches on the wire will now be held in front of the stitches that you have just worked).

5 Thread the stitches along the wire so that both sets of stitches are sitting on the needle ends, and pull the back tip through to put the back stitches on the wire. Repeat from *.

'Magic Loop'

This technique was first devised by Sarah Hauschka; some people advise that you should use a circular needle with a long cable such as an 80 or even 100cm length, and no shorter. However, all lengths of circular needle are suitable except for the very short, although around 100cm does work particularly well for socks. If you have an abundance of circular needles to choose from, then it is worth taking the time to sift through your collection for those that have relatively short needle tips and a smooth join between the wire and the needle tip.

Cast the required number of stitches onto the circular needle using your preferred method. (It is easier to work with an even number of stitches although this is not essential.)

1 Count out half the stitches and place a marker between the two sets. Push the stitches down onto the wire and fold in half at the marked point.

2 Pinch the cable and pull it through the stitches at this point so that half the stitches are on either side of the folded wire.

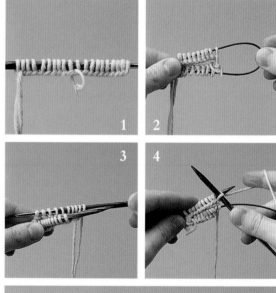

Avoiding a ladder

Many knitters find that they achieve a looser tension on the final stitch knitted from one needle and the first stitch knitted from the second needle (or at the point where the cable is pulled through when using the 'Magic Loop' method). This uneven tension can create a ladder and is common when knitting on circular needles or sets of double-pointed needles **(1)**.

Many tutorials will advise that you make sure you work a really tight stitch when starting work on a new set of stitches. However, this can often over-compensate for the loose tension and cause an over-tight stitch which in turn makes the stitch either side of it seem baggy.

With both the two needle method and the 'Magic Loop' method you can create an even tension by slipping the last stitch worked from the back needle onto the new needle tip before you start working on the next set of stitches **(2 + 3)**.

TIP: If you haven't enjoyed using circular needles in the past, it is worth knowing that they have improved enormously over the last decade and many now exist with beautifully smooth cable-to-tip joins and flexible cables. Both 'Magic Loop' and using two circular needles are methods for knitting small numbers of stitches in the round. However, if you don't enjoy either of these, then don't forget that instead you can use double-pointed needles (DPNs) for small diameter knitting.

Inside out?

You may find after a few rows that you have the wrong side of your work facing you. For example, when working stocking stitch you find that the purl side of the fabric is facing you and that the knit side is on the inside of your tubular piece of knitting. This is because – in your excitement at how great these techniques are – you have changed direction and knitted across the back set of stitches and left the front set on the wire rather than knitting the front set and leaving the back set of stitches on the wire, when holding them in the left hand.

When working a tubular piece that has an open end, such as a mitten or a sock, you can correct this by simply turning your knitting 'inside out' so that the right side of the fabric is facing you. However, if you have done this when knitting a finger of a glove, for example, you will have no choice but to unpick.

Dealing with wayward wires

If circular needles are stored curled in a loop for a while (especially those with a long connecting cable) you may find it hard to uncurl the wire. This can mean that you struggle to keep the wires under control and can lead to you mistakenly twisting your knitted stitches or looping the yarn around the needle wire whilst working your stitches.

To prevent your wayward wires from making things tricky, simply submerge the cables in a bowl of very hot water for half an hour. Then leave to dry and cool off in a straight position (you may want to weigh them down so that they stay put).

COMBINATION KNITTING
Annie Modesitt

While there are many ways to create knitted fabric (one count has 16 as the magic number of different ways to form a knit stitch), there are basically three major styles of knitting in the world today; Western, Eastern and Combination.

Here we are using the term style of knitting to describe how a stitch is actually formed, not the way a knitter holds their yarn while creating the stitch. Whether held in the left hand (Continental), or the right hand (English) (see page 154), or even around the neck (Portuguese) a knitter can use any style of knitting to create their fabric.

Eastern knitting

The least common knitting style is Eastern knitting (1), which creates a fabric where every stitch is criss-crossed, creating a denser and thicker fabric with less elasticity than traditional knit fabric.

Eastern may be the oldest form of knitting, most closely resembling nailbinding (a needle craft which uses an eyed needle and a finite length of fibre). Eastern stitches are twisted, which creates a very firm fabric.

The origin of Eastern knitting seems to be the area around the Mediterranean and the Near East, although pockets of this type of knitting are presently found in South America.

Western knitting

Western knitting is the most common style (2), and has come to be considered the standard style of knitting around the world. Western knitting is generally found in parts of the world culturally influenced by Northern and Western Europe. It is worked with the leading edge of both the knit and the purl stitch to the front of the needle, and the yarn is wrapped around the working needle from back to front for both stitches.

The term 'working needle' describes the needle that does most of the work, entering the stitch which sits on the 'resting needle'. For most knitters, the working needle is the right-hand needle, but in various situations (left-handed and 'backwards' knitting) the left needle may be the working needle.

One truism of all knitting is that the way the stitch is wrapped in the previous row directly impacts the way the stitch is mounted in the current row. In Western knitting, the knit and purl stitches are mounted in the same direction on the knitting needle.

Combination knitting

In Combination knitting, the knit and purl stitches are seated differently on the needle.

This discrepancy happens because the Combination purl (3) is wrapped differently as it is formed, and therefore in the following row the Combination knit is mounted so that the leading edge is facing towards the tip.

This means that the working needle goes through the back loop (4) or leg of the stitch when entering the Combination knit stitch rather than through the front (5). Once the needle is in the stitch, the Combination knit stitch is wrapped in the same way as the Western knit stitch.

Combination knitting roots

Although less common as a style, Combination knitting creates a fabric that is identical to Western knit fabric.

As with many folk crafts, hard data on the genesis of Combination knitting isn't available. Our best guess is that maverick knitters created their own form of knitting, only to discover how well it blended beautifully with more established styles. The Combination knitters we've come across are often taught by grandparents of Hungarian ancestry. Perhaps in areas where Eastern and Western cultures mingled, clever and resourceful knitters found a way to use the best of both methods in their knitting style.

Benefits of Combination knitting

We find that this method of knitting is intuitive, much easier on the hands with less wrist strain, and creates a beautiful tension with less 'rowing out', because both the knit and purl stitches are created using the same amount of yarn.

In Western knitting, the purl stitch (6) uses a bit more yarn as it travels over the needle. In Combination knitting, the purl stitch uses essentially the same amount of yarn as the knit stitch. If a knitter is able to relax their hands as they knit and purl, the tension of the fabric will be very even.

Because it's necessary to pull the purl a bit tighter when knitting Western style, often a Western knitter may experience rowing out (7) when first attempting Combination knitting, with different tension on knit and purl rows affecting evenness, particularly in stocking stitch.

The easiest way we've found to relax while setting tension is to NOT pull or hold the yarn tightly while a stitch is being formed. After the stitch is seated on the working needle, enter the next stitch and at that point give a tiny tug on the yarn while working the next stitch. This will tighten the stitch previously worked, forming it to the exact size of the needle and setting perfect tension. When the hands are not enmeshed in a 'cat's cradle' of tensioning yarn, they can relax and knitting can be more joyful.

One of the nicest things about Combination knitting is the fact that the knit and purl stitches are mounted differently on the needle. This allows the knitter to 'read' their knitting much more easily than with Western knitting.

Diagnosing a knitting problem is the first step in correcting the error and learning not to make it again. Combination knitting allows one to read and diagnose problems more easily, creating a more intuitive knitter.

Stitch mounts and ribbing

The difference in stitch mounts can be most clearly seen in Western **(8)** and Combination ribbing **(9)**. Because the knits and purls are mounted differently on the needle in Combination, there's no need to count, or even look, at ribbing to form the correct columns of knits and purls.

When to use Combination knitting

You may prefer to use Combination knitting for all your straight plain knitting. This allows the maximum benefit of the Combination purl to create fabric which closely resembles plain knitting worked in the round.

When working plain knitting in the round, or knitting garter stitch back and forth, the stitches are seated in the Western fashion, so that is the style you may prefer to use in those particular cases.

Rethinking knitting instructions

By teaching beginning knitting students how to knit and purl in the same class, they grasp the similarities between these techniques. One stitch informs how the other will be made, and that reinforces the understanding that a purl stitch is simply the inverse of a knit stitch.

There are only two main differences to consider when working a traditional knitting pattern in Combination style: decreases and twisted stitches.

Decreases

One of the main benefits of Combination knitting is that the knitter is very aware of how the knit and purl stitches are seated on the needle. For this reason, the concept of left- and right-slanting decreases seems to be easier to understand and visualise.

Knitting decreases fall into three categories: left slanting, right slanting or vertical. With the exception of vertical decreases (which must contain an odd number of stitches), a decrease can contain any number of stitches.

In traditional knitting patterns the term K2tog (knit 2 together) means 'knit 2 stitches together so they slant to the right' and SSK (slip, slip, knit) means 'rearrange the stitches so they can be knit together to slant to the left'.

For this reason you may prefer to use the terms K2tog-R and K2tog-L to describe these two outcomes, and leave it up to the knitter to choose the best technique to accomplish it.

Since Combination knits are seated differently from Western knits, they must be re-seated when forming a K2tog-R, as they cannot be knitted through the back of the loop **(10)**. The stitches must be turned around so they face away from the tip of the needle. To do this, slip the 2 stitches by lifting them off the left-hand needle through the back of the loop **(11)**. They will now be seated correctly on the right-hand needle **(12)**. Then slip them back to the left-hand needle, and knit them together through the front of the loop **(13)**.

However, when forming a left-slanting decrease Combination knits are perfectly aligned for a K2tog-L (aka SSK) so no rearranging is necessary **(14)**.

A VDD (vertical double decrease) reduces three stitches down to one, leaving the centre stitch as the final stitch remaining. This gives a strong vertical line. The easiest way to work this is to slip 2 stitches as if to work a K2tog-R, knit the next stitch **(15)**, then pass the slipped stitches over the knit stitch **(16)**.

Twisted stitches

When patterns call for a knitter to K1 tbl (knit 1 through the back loop), it is asking the knitter to twist the stitch. A better way to think of this technique would be, 'knit 1 through the trailing edge' – or simply twist the stitch. Each stitch has a leading and a trailing edge. The leading edge is the side of the stitch which 'wants' the needle to enter it – it is more welcoming. When the working needle enters a stitch through the leading edge, the stitch opens up and embraces the tip of the needle.

The trailing edge is the side of the stitch where the yarn is wrapped around the needle tip to make a stitch. If the stitch is a doorway, the trailing edge would be the exit. When a working needle enters a stitch through the trailing edge, not only is it a tighter fit (it just doesn't feel right), but the two legs of the stitch can also be seen to be crossed at the bottom of the stitch **(17)**.

When switching between Western and Combination knitting, or when first learning one technique after mastering the other, it's important to pay close attention to the base of the stitch to be sure you are not inadvertently twisting it.

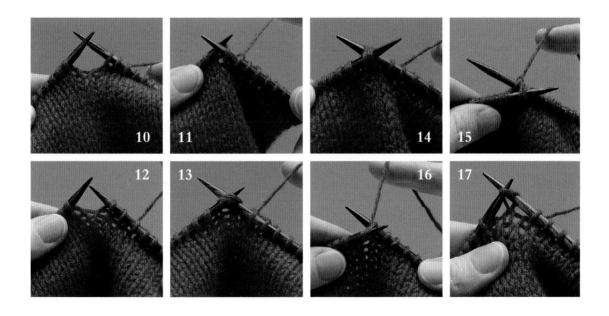

NEXUS SOCKS

Jon Dunn-Ballam

Combine cables and openwork in this fascinating men's sock pattern, ideal for showing off a hand-dyed yarn.

Inspired by designer Jon Dunn-Ballam's dyeing adventures, his Nexus pattern is a delightful challenge. He says, 'When I first dyed my Superwash Merino Cashmere Mix yarn in the Aztec colourway, I was instantly reminded of sands as they slip through an hourglass. The "bricky", delicate tones of deserts and sandstone structures came to mind. And so Nexus was born, combining my love of cables with some subtle, yet striking, openwork.'

Nexus is a real pleasure to knit in this luscious, soft yarn, which is available in 11 hand-dyed shades.

SIZE

	S	M	L	
Ankle	22	23½	25	cm
Circumference	8½	9½	10	in

Sock height and foot length are fully adjustable while knitting the pattern

YARN
Easyknits Cherish (4ply weight; 80% superwash merino, 10% cashmere, 10% nylon; 400m/100g skeins)
Aztec 1 x 100g skein for all sizes

NEEDLES & ACCESSORIES
1 set of 2.5mm (UK 13–12/US 1–2) double-pointed needles or circular needles, 80cm long, in same size for knitting using 'Magic Loop' technique (see page 44)
Cable needle (cn), stitch marker, stitch holder

TENSION
40 sts to 10cm over unstretched twisted rib pattern using 2.5mm needles
36 sts and 48 rounds to 10cm over unstretched leg pattern using 2.5mm needles
30 sts to 10cm over stretched leg pattern using 2.5mm needles

SPECIAL ABBREVIATIONS
T2B: Slip next stitch to cn and hold at back of work, K1, then P1 from cn
T2F: Slip next stitch to cn and hold at front of work, P1, then K1 from cn

Stitch patterns

1x1 twisted rib pattern
Rnd 1: *K1 tbl, P1. Repeat from * to end of round.
Repeat this round.

Lace cable pattern
Worked over 7 sts and 6 rounds.
Rnd 1: P2, yo, Sl 1, K2tog, psso, yo, P2.
Rnd 2: P2, K3, P2.
Rnd 3: P2, K1, yo, SSK, P2.
Rnds 4, 5 & 6: P2, K3, P2.

Wave pattern
Worked over 8 sts and 16 rounds.
Rnd 1: P3, K2, P3.
Rnd 2 and all even numbered rnds: Purl the purl sts
and slip the knit sts.
Rnd 3: P2, T2B, T2F, P2.
Rnd 5: P1, T2B, P2, T2F, P1.
Rnd 7: T2B, P4, T2F.
Rnd 9: T2F, P4, T2B.
Rnd 11: P1, T2F, P2, T2B, P1.
Rnd 13: P2, T2F, T2B, P2.
Rnd 15: P3, K2, P3.
Rnd 16: As rnd 2.

Sock

Using 2.5mm circular needles or DPNs cast on 68 (72: 76)
sts using a stretchy cast on method. Divide sts evenly
between desired needles (working on a circular needle
with the 'Magic Loop' method can help with complex
patterns, as you simply divide the stitches between front
and back).

Join to work in the round, being careful not to twist
your sts. Place a marker for the beginning of the round.

Cuff
Work 16 (18: 20) rnds in 1x1 twisted rib pattern.
Purl 2 rnds.

LEG PATTERN
Small only
Rnd 1: Slm, P1, K1 tbl, Lace Cable rnd 1, K1 tbl, P1, Wave
rnd 1, P1, K1 tbl, Lace Cable rnd 1, K1 tbl, P1, Wave rnd 1,
P1, K1 tbl, P1, Lace Cable rnd 1, P2, Lace Cable rnd 1, P1,
K1 tbl, P1, Wave rnd 1.

Medium only

Rnd 1: Slm, P1, K1 tbl, P1, Lace Cable rnd 1, P1, K1 tbl, P1, Wave rnd 1, P1, K1 tbl, P1, Lace Cable rnd 1, P1, K1 tbl, P1, Wave rnd 1, P1, K1 tbl, P1, Lace Cable rnd 1, P2, Lace Cable rnd 1, P1, K1 tbl, P1, Wave rnd 1.

Large only

Rnd 1: Slm, P1, K1 tbl, P1, Lace Cable rnd 1, P1, K1 tbl, P1, Wave rnd 1, P1, K1 tbl, P1, Lace Cable rnd 1, P1, K1 tbl, P1, Wave rnd 1, P1, K1 tbl, P1, Lace Cable rnd 1, P1, K1 tbl, P2, K1 tbl, P1, Lace Cable rnd 1, P1, K1 tbl, P1, Wave rnd 1.

All sizes

Continue to work as set, using appropriate rnd of stitch patterns, until sock is approx 10cm less than your desired cuff to heel measurement. Sock photographed measures 17cm at this point (cuff to heel is 27cm).

PATTERN MOVEMENT
Small only

Next rnd: Slm, [P1, K1 tbl, P2, P2tog, P3, K1 tbl, P1], pm, Wave, pm, [P1, K1 tbl, P3, P2tog, P2, K1 tbl, P1], pm, Wave, P1, K1 tbl, M1, P1, Lace Cable, P2, Lace Cable, P1, M1, K1 tbl, P1, Wave.

Medium only

Next rnd: Slm, [P1, K1 tbl, P4, P2tog, P3, K1 tbl, P1], pm, Wave, pm, [P1, K1 tbl, P4, P2tog, P3, K1 tbl, P1], pm, Wave, P1, K1 tbl, M1, P1, Lace Cable, P2, Lace Cable, P1, M1, K1 tbl, P1, Wave.

Large only

Next rnd: Slm, [P1, K1 tbl, P4, P2tog, P3, K1 tbl, P1], pm, Wave, pm, [P1, K1 tbl, P4, P2tog, P3, K1 tbl, P1], pm, Wave, P1, K1 tbl, M1, P1, Lace Cable, P1, K1 tbl, P2, K1 tbl, P1, Lace Cable, P1, M1, K1 tbl, P1, Wave.

All sizes

Decreases and increases as set above are worked on alt rounds until all sts between the two sets of markers (also shown in square brackets) have been removed. Work a single decrease in the centre of each of the two marked sections, keeping the twisted stitches correct until they meet and are also removed. Cont to inc 1 st on each side of the two remaining lace cable patterns. Inc sts are taken into rev st st. The overall stitch count does not change.

After final inc and dec round, work partial round as folls:
Next rnd: Slm, Wave, Wave, P1, K1 tbl, P12 (14: 14), Lace Cable, P0 (0: 1), K0 (0: 1) tbl, P2, K0 (0: 1) tbl, P0 (0: 1), Lace Cable, P9 (10: 9).

Remove start of rnd marker, and place new marker at point just reached. It should be 5 (6: 7) sts before the first wave motif.

Work across instep sts as folls: Slm, P3 (4: 5), K1 tbl, P1, Wave, Wave, Wave, P1, K1 tbl, P3 (4: 5) and place these on a spare needle or stitch holder.

Heel

The rem 34 (36: 38) sts will form the heel flap. Work in rows as foll:
Row 1: *Sl 1, K1; rep from * to end.
Row 2: Sl 1, purl to end.
Repeat these 2 rows 14 (15: 16) more times.
You should be able to count 15 (16: 17) slipped sts down each side of the heel flap at this point.

Turning the heel

Row 1: K19 (20: 21), K2tog tbl, K1, turn, leaving 12 (13: 14) sts unworked.
Row 2: Sl 1, P5, P2tog, P1, turn.
Row 3: Sl 1, knit until you are 1 st away from the gap formed by previous turn, K2tog tbl, K1, turn.
Row 4: Sl 1, purl to 1 st before gap, P2tog, P1, turn.
Rep last 2 rows until all sts are used up, ending with a plain knit row.

Gusset

Resume working in the round as foll: Using the slipped sts at the edge of the heel flap, pick up and knit 15 (16: 17) sts up the side of the flap, pm, work in patt across instep sts from holder, pick up and K15 (16: 17) sts down the other side of the heel flap and knit to marker.
Rnd 1: Work across instep sts in patt, knit across heel sts to 3 sts before marker, K2tog, K1.
Rnd 2: Work across instep sts in patt, K1, SSK, knit to marker.
Repeat these 2 rounds until you have decreased to 68 (72: 76) sts, ensuring wave pattern is maintained on instep.

Foot

Rnd 1: Slm, P3 (4:5), K1 tbl, P1, Wave, Wave, Wave, P1, K1 tbl, P3 (4:5), pm, knit to end of round.

Cont working the pattern as set until the sock, measured from heel to needles, meas 4½ (5:5½)cm less than desired foot length.

Toe shaping

Rnd 1: Slm, knit to marker, slm, knit to end.

Rnd 2: Slm, K1, K2tog, knit to 3 sts before marker, SSK, K1, slm, K1, K2tog, knit to 3 sts before marker, SSK, K1. 64 (68:72) sts.

Repeat these 2 rnds until 28 sts rem.

Grafting toe

Slip 14 instep sts to one needle and 14 sole stitches to another needle. Graft these sts together using Kitchener stitch.

Weave in all loose ends and cast on straight away for second sock.

4 CABLES

Creating intricate textures and meandering shapes in your knitting is part of the joy of cables. It really isn't a complicated technique, but with that extra needle and all the charts it can seem quite daunting. Our masterclass has been selected to help you get the most out of your cables.

LIBERATE YOUR CABLES
Jane Crowfoot

One thing that can put even experienced knitters off cabling is the prospect of juggling a third needle. But just because cable needles exist in all shapes and sizes, it doesn't mean that they're always necessary. For those of you who are new to knitting or for anyone who's working with a chunky yarn, cabling can actually be easier if it's done without the use of a cable needle. It not only frees up your hands, but it also speeds up the production of your cables. And many people say they find that cabling without a special needle makes their cables neater too.

Cabling basically means working stitches out of order and can be done with two ordinary knitting needles. Cabling in this way can be done with any kind of yarn – a great way to try out the technique first is to use a medium- or heavyweight yarn. The only circumstance in which cabling without a special needle could get tricky is if you've got very large numbers of stitches to move, but otherwise, it's a technique that you really should have a go at.

Over the next few pages we'll give you a brief guide to cables, and then full step-by-step instructions to working a cable without a cable needle, which even those who are new to knitting will be able to follow. Then, if you want to explore the technique further, we'll explain how you can adapt it to work other kinds of cables.

Cable needles

What is a cable needle used for?

Cables are sections of knitting where the stitches are worked out of order. A cable needle is used to hold stitches while a cable is being twisted. When working from a pattern you'll be told to place a determined number of stitches onto the cable needle in order to hold them at the front or the back of the work while the stitches that remain on the knitting needle are worked on.

Where should I hold my stitches?

The place at which you hold the stitches (either at the front or the back of the work) will influence the shape of your cable. Stitches held at the front will create a cable which has stitches crossed to the left hand side on the front of the work. We will refer to this as a cable that leads to the left. Stitches held at the back will create a cable that has stitches crossed to the right-hand side on the front of the work. We will refer to this as a cable that leads to the right.

In standard patterns the stitch terminology will refer to 'B' for stitches held at the back and 'F' for stitches held at the front (sometimes also referred to as 'R' and 'L'). The letter 'C' stands for cable. Where the letter 'T' is used, this usually indicates that some stitches will be purled rather than knitted, and stands for twist.

Working a cable without a cable needle

You may find it easier to use a medium- to heavyweight yarn to start with. Here, we'll show you two different cables worked without the use of a cable needle:

A cable that leads to the left (C4F):

1   Work to where the stitches need to be crossed. With the yarn held to the reverse of the work, slip the next 2 stitches purlwise.

2   Carry the yarn across the back of the 2 slipped stitches and knit the next 2 stitches from the left needle.

3   Insert the left needle through the front of the 2 slipped stitches on the right-hand needle.

4   Carefully pull the right-hand needle out of all 4 stitches (2 slipped and 2 knitted), allowing the 2 knitted stitches to drop off the needle, while transferring the slipped stitches to the left needle. It is a good idea to pinch underneath the 2 loose stitches using your left hand.

5   Insert the right needle purlwise into the 2 dropped stitches.

6   Knit the next 2 stitches, thus completing the cable.

7   As you can see, the cable leads to the left. This becomes more obvious once the next row has been worked.

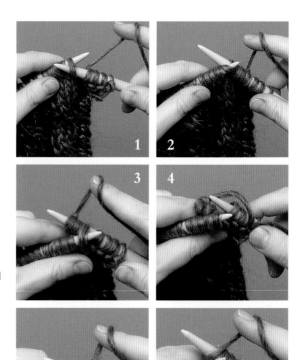

A cable that leads to the right (C4B):

8 Work to where the stitches need to be crossed. With the yarn held to the front of the work, slip the next 2 stitches purlwise.

9 Carry the yarn across the front of the 2 stitches. Hold the yarn at the back and knit the next 2 stitches from the left needle, keeping the tension firm.

10 Insert the left needle down through the back of the 2 slipped stitches on the right needle.

11 Carefully allow the 2 knitted stitches to drop off the needle, while transferring the slipped stitches to the left needle. It's a good idea to pinch the 2 dropped stitches using your left hand.

12 Insert the right needle purlwise into the 2 dropped stitches.

13 Knit the next 2 stitches, thus completing the cable.

14 The cable now leads to the right. This will become more obvious once the next row has been worked.

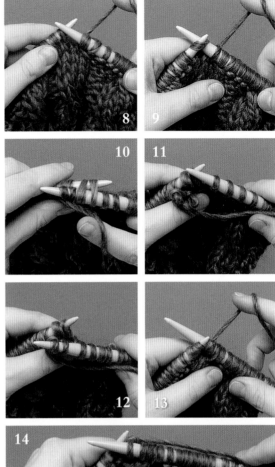

Other types of cable

Knitting patterns call for many different types of cable. The technique illustrated here can be simply adjusted to suit the instructions given.

Change the number of stitches that you slip to match the number put on the cable needle, ensuring that the yarn is at the back of the work if the cable needle should be held at front, and vice versa.

Then work the following stitches as instructed (purl, knit or other combinations, such as twists).

Retrieve the slipped stitches as shown above,

depending on whether the instructions were for a back or front cable, and work them as instructed.

In the case of the Baird Collar (see page 62), for example, you will see that 4 stitches are moved to make the cable and 2 stitches are purled to create the background of reverse stocking stitch.

Liberating yourself from the cable needle makes this type of project much easier to work on the go. You no longer need to worry about dropping the needle between cables or losing it altogether. Many of the best-known designers never use a cable needle, so why not give it a go and join them?

CONFIDENT CABLES
Belinda Boaden

Cable charts are a relatively new phenomenon, only becoming popular in the last twenty years or so. However, following a pictorial set of instructions for cables makes sense, in much the same way as charts for intarsia do. Rather than long, written instructions for each row, a good chart shows exactly how your cables should look. Once you've worked one full pattern repeat, your knitting itself can become your chart – making knitting easier as you're not having to constantly refer to a book or photocopy of the pattern.

Reading cable charts

Let's start by looking at a simple cable chart **(1)**. As with all charts, each square represents a stitch, so this is a cable panel of 8 stitches and 16 rows. While at first glance it might look complicated, it's a compound cable made up of one of the most basic cables you will ever come across: a 2-stitch over 2-stitch cross either backwards or forwards. Written out, row 3 (the first row where you need to work cables) would be:

Slip the next 2 stitches to cable needle and hold at the back, K2, K2 from cable needle, slip the next 2 stitches to cable needle and hold at the front, K2, K2 from cable needle.

This could then be abbreviated to 'C4B, C4F' if the written instructions are given at the beginning of the pattern. Even then, if you're not an experienced knitter it might be hard to visualise exactly what it is meant to look like once knitted, and also it can be daunting to see a whole row of 100-plus stitches written in this manner.

Drawn out as a chart, it's clear to see how for C4B, the first 2 stitches appear to be moved behind the second 2, as the diagonal lines move from bottom left to upper right from the second set of stitches across the first set, showing you that the second set of 2 stitches needs to move over the front of the first set of stitches. With C4F, the diagonal lines showing the stitch movement draw the eye from bottom right to upper left, making it look like the first set of 2 stitches is moving across and in front of the second set.

Knitted up, you can now see how this looks **(2)**, and how the chart visualises the cable for you.

If you have trouble with the black–and–whiteness of the charts, it's very simple to use highlighter pens and allocate each cable symbol a colour, giving you an even more visual cipher for your knitting **(3)**.

Let's move on now to a chart with purl stitches **(4)**. Not only are we dealing with purl stitches, but also with non-symmetrical cables, where 2 stitches are moved over 1 stitch only, and that stitch needs to be a purl stitch to make the reverse stocking stitch background within the panel. Written out, row 3 would be:

(Slip the next 2 stitches to cable needle and hold at front, P1, K2 from cable needle), P2, repeat ( ), [slip the next stitch to cable needle and hold at back, K2, P1 from cable needle], P2, repeat [ ].

This could be abbreviated to 'T3F, P2, T3F, T3B, P2, T3B', but perhaps with even fewer clues as to what your finished row would look like than the 'C4B, C4F'.

The chart, however, clearly shows how the knit stitches set up in rows 1 and 2 move across the background purl stitches, shown by dots in the chart. It is the standard

convention to use a blank square in a chart to show that the stitch is knitted on the RS of the work, and purled on the WS, and a dot to show a purl on the RS and a knit on the WS.

Knitted up **(5)**, chart 4 begins to look quite recognisable, and highlighted **(6)** you can see where the C4F from chart A also comes into play on row 5.

If cables are comprised only of ordinary knit and purl stitches, then the basics described above work on all charts. Like many things in knitting, it's often a lot easier to do than to explain, so we would encourage anyone to try a cable chart at least once, even if until now you've been a dyed-in-the-wool written instruction person. All good charts should have a key with written instructions to get you going; even if they haven't, though, a few minutes of study and a couple of highlighter pens should be enough to break down the most complicated chart into components that can be easily understood.

KEY

☐ K on RS, P on WS

▣ P on RS, K on WS

▨ T3B

◣ T3F

▧ C4B

◺ C4F

▢ Row pattern repeat

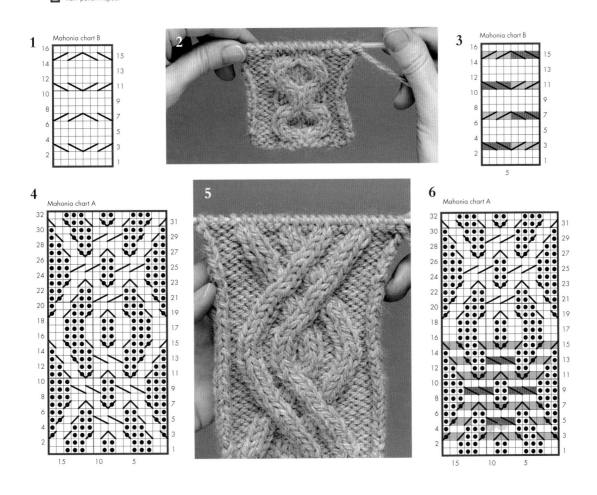

Twisted stitch cable charts

Some cables, of course, use twisted stitches or other non-standard stitches, and so for this you will see purl stitches charted within cables (7). Here there are no 'blank' knit stitches, but there is a loop symbol. This is to show that all stitches are knitted through the back of the loop; they are even twisted when working a cable. Although the chart looks complicated, there are really only two different cables here: one where 2 twisted stitches are passed over each other (1 st over 1 st) either backwards or forwards, and one where a twisted stitch is moved right or left over a background purl stitch as highlighted. So, written out, row 4 read left to right would be:

P1, (slip next stitch to cable needle and hold at front, P1, K1 tbl from cable needle, slip next stitch to cable needle and hold at back, K1 tbl, P1 from cable needle), P2, K1 tbl, P5, slip next stitch to cable needle and hold at back, K1 tbl, P1 from cable needle, slip next stitch to cable needle and hold at front, P1, K1 tbl from cable needle, P5, K1 tbl, P2, repeat ( ), P1.

Rather lengthy, isn't it? Especially if you imagine writing out all 24 rows of this chart – and again, it's remarkably unclear as to what the knitting will actually look like.

The chart, on the other hand, gives you an idea of the row you're about to knit, and helps you to see the pattern developing as you go. You can also avoid mistakes before you've gone so far that they involve much unravelling.

Fixing mistakes in cables

1   Despair need not be a factor in cables, however, even if you do discover a mistake several rows or even patterns back. Here, from our original chart 1 on page 59, the first cable on row 7 has been worked as a C4B instead of a C4F, but it's not been noticed until row 13. In a garment this could mean unravelling more than a thousand stitches, but there is an alternative. It helps here if you have a spare cable needle as well as the one you're using, and an old machine knitting needle or latch-hook needle is very, very useful, although a crochet hook can be used.

2   Work your next row (row 13) until you reach the cable stitches, then drop the next 4 stitches of the cable off the LH needle and unravel them down to the offending cable.

3   Now put the first 2 stitches onto one cable needle and the second 2 stitches onto another.

4   Reposition the cable needles so that the cable is twisted the correct way, and slip them all onto one cable needle.

7   KEY   ● P on RS

   ⊼ K1 tbl

   Sl 1 to cn and hold at front, P1; K1 tbl from cn

   Sl 1 to cn and hold at back, K1 tbl; P1 from cn

   Sl 1 to cn and hold at back, K1 tbl; K1 tbl from cn

   Sl 1 to cn and hold at front, K1 tbl; K1 tbl from cn

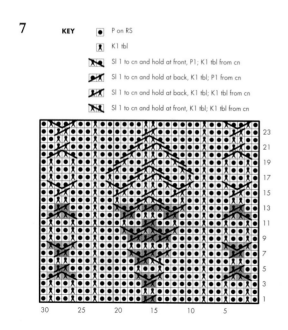

5+6 Now you need to re-knit them using the bar of yarn unravelled from the row above, so with the (now spare again) cable needle, knit these 4 stitches. This is a little bit fiddly, but do-able.

7+8 Now you can use your latch-hook needle or crochet hook to work the plain rows up to where you need to re-cable the cable on row 11, so work the first stitch on your cable needle up the rows and then hold it on your spare cable needle. Repeat for the remaining three stitches.

9 Once again, split the stitches onto your two cable needles, position them so that the cable is twisting the correct way, slip them all onto one cable needle and re-knit that row. You are left with one 'bar' of yarn from the first row you unravelled (row 12) to knit these 4 stitches with and then you can carry on with row 13 as if nothing untoward had happened.

10 Your reworked cable might look a little wobbly, but it is easy to even the stitches out by teasing them with a needle. If they still look uneven after that, by the time the garment is blocked, steamed and being worn it is highly unlikely to be noticeable.

Avoiding baggy stitches

Another problem some people have with cables is that the last stitch of the cable is often slightly looser than the first stitch of the reverse stocking stitch background, and looks a little baggy. This does not seem to happen to everybody, and again in some cases is remedied when the stitches even themselves out with the first wash or when they're wet blocked.

Another solution is to knit until you are ready to cast off your knitting, work to the purl stitch after the offending stitch and drop it down to a few rows above the beginning of your cable (best not to go right to the very bottom unless you are very brave). Turn your work over so that the WS is facing you and the purl stitch you just dropped now has its knit side facing you (it's easier to pick up knit stitches than purl stitches), take your latch hook or crochet hook and re-knit up all the rows, giving each stitch a bit of a tug to take up some of the slack from that baggy knit stitch.

Or, for slightly less effort, try to knit that last stitch of your cable a bit tighter on each row; just give your yarn a bit of a tug as you bring it to the front of the work to work the next purl stitch.

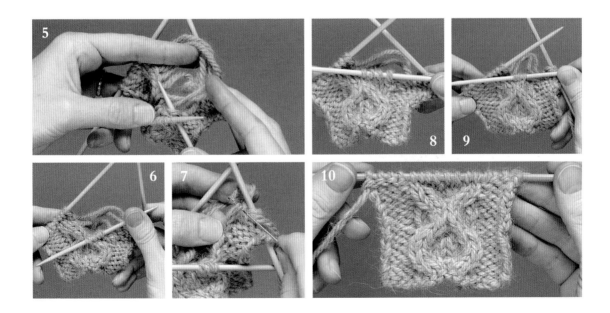

BAIRD COLLAR
Jeanette Sloan

Create this chunky cabled collar with a statement button as the perfect finishing touch for your winter outfits.

Wrap up warm and look stylish with this cabled collar, worked in gorgeous Lang Mille Colori yarn. This is a quick-to-knit project, but one that involves several techniques to keep it interesting. There's short-row shaping at the back of the neck to make it lie beautifully, and the collar is knitted in two pieces and grafted together using Kitchener stitch. It would also be a good pattern for anyone wanting to try cabling without a cable needle.

Designer Jeanette Sloan says, 'I wanted to create a statement accessory that was more than simply a scarf but didn't involve complicated shaping. Short-row shaping creates the rise in the ribbing which allows the design to fit snugly into the back of the neck, feeling like a big woolly hug!'

The Lang Mille Colori yarn has beautiful texture and variegated colour with tones of moss and heather. Jeanette used it doubled for her design to get a chunky feel. She offers a word of advice: 'Remember when grafting the pieces together for the main section that there are both knit and purl stitches to graft. Reverse the way the darning needle enters the purl stitches in order to achieve an invisible graft.'

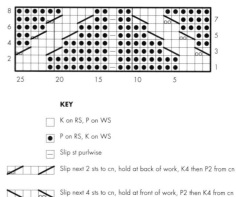

KEY

☐ K on RS, P on WS

⬤ P on RS, K on WS

☐ Slip st purlwise

Slip next 2 sts to cn, hold at back of work, K4 then P2 from cn

Slip next 4 sts to cn, hold at front of work, P2 then K4 from cn

Pattern

Make two pieces alike.
Using 10mm needles and yarn doubled, cast on 25 sts.
Row 1 (RS): (K1, P1) to last st, K1.
Row 2: (P1, K1) to last st, P1.
Repeat these 2 rows once more.

Change to 12mm needles and starting at bottom right of chart work 8-row cable pattern 5 times then place all sts on holder.

Finishing and making up

Graft both sets of sts together using Kitchener Stitch then weave in all ends.

Neck rib

Turn piece so that RS is facing. Use 10mm needles and yarn doubled to pick up and knit 57 sts into long side edge starting at right cast-on edge of rib and ending at left cast-on edge of rib.

Work 3 rows in 1x1 rib as before, then begin short row shaping of rib as foll:
Row 1: Rib to last 5 sts, w&t.
Row 2: As row 1.
Row 3: Rib to last 12 sts, w&t.
Row 4: As row 3.
Row 5: Rib to last 19 sts, w&t.
Row 6: As row 5.
Next row: Rib 17 then break off yarn.

Slip all sts onto same needle then rejoin yarn and rib across all sts working wraps with wrapped stitches as you go. Cast off in rib then weave in all remaining ends.

Again using yarn doubled, make a button loop at the base of the rib on the right rib edge making sure it is large enough for the button to pass through. Using the photograph as a guide, position button so that it corresponds to the button loop and sew in place.

SIZE
28cm x 70cm (11in x 27½in)

YARN
Lang Yarns Mille Colori Big (50% new wool, 50% acrylic; 190m/200g balls)
Shade 757.0024: 2 x 200g balls used doubled throughout

NEEDLES & ACCESSORIES
1 pair 12mm (US 17) knitting needles
1 pair 10mm (UK 000/US 15) knitting needles
1 x 45mm wooden button
Large eyed darning needle

TENSION
8 sts and 13 rows to 10cm over st st using 12mm needles and yarn doubled

STITCHES
W&t: Wrap and turn. Take yarn between needles to opposite side of work, slip next stitch, take yarn between needles to other side of work, pass same slipped stitch back to right needle, turn work

PATTERN NOTES
The main part of the collar is worked in two pieces that are grafted together at the centre using Kitchener stitch

CABLE CUSHION COVERS
Amanda Crawford

**Indulge in some luxury for your home with these soft
cushions featuring sumptuous cables and bobbles.**

These soft, luxurious and highly detailed cable
cushions would look wonderful on any sofa or
armchair, particularly if you knit the whole set.
They've been designed for us by Amanda
Crawford, who was inspired by vintage patterns.
'Their stitches are so much more interesting and
more complex than today's designs,' Amanda says.
'I like knitting with different stitches and making
interesting textures.'

The three cushions are knitted in Sublime's
Cashmere Merino Silk Aran, a smooth, high-
quality yarn. Each cushion has its own
combination of cable and bobble patterns, with
different fastenings on the back – covered
buttons, i-cords and tie-backs – to provide an
eye-catching finishing detail to each cushion.

If you've never knitted bobbles before, these
patterns are ideal for developing your skills and
perfecting your technique.

I-cord button version

PANEL A
Worked over 18 sts and 1 row:
Row 1: [P1, K1] 9 times.

PANEL B
Worked over 9 sts and 8 rows:
Row 1 (RS): C4B, K1, C4F.
Row 2: P9.

SIZE
40cm x 40cm (16in x 16in)

YARN
Sirdar Sublime Cashmere Merino Silk Aran (75% extra fine merino,
20% silk, 5% cashmere; 86/50g balls)
Sprout (19) 6 x 50g balls

NEEDLES & ACCESSORIES
1 pair 4.5mm (UK 7/US 7) knitting needles
1 pair 4.5mm (UK 7/US 7) double-pointed needles (for i-cord)
Cable needle
Cushion pad 40cm x 40cm

SPECIAL ABBREVIATIONS
C4B: Slip 2 sts onto cable needle and hold at back of work, K2 then
K2from cable needle
C4F: Slip 2 sts onto cable needle and hold at front of work, K2, then K2
from cable needle.
MB: Make bobble by knitting into next stitch 5 times, turn, P5, turn, K5,
turn, P2tog, P1, P2tog, turn, K3tog
T3B: Slip 1 st onto cable needle and hold at back of work, K2, P1 from
cable needle
T3F: Slip 2 sts onto cable needle and hold at front of work, P1, K2 from
cable needle
T4B: Slip 2 sts onto cable needle and hold at back of work, K2, P2 from
cable needle
T4F: Slip 2 sts onto cable needle and hold at front of work, P2, K2 from
cable needle

Row 3: K4, MB, K4.

Row 4: P9.

Row 5: K3, MB, K1, MB, K3.

Row 6: P9.

Row 7: K9.

Row 8: P9.

PANEL C

Worked over 24 sts and 16 rows:

Row 1 (RS): P2, C4B, [P4, C4B] twice, P2.

Row 2: K2, P4, [K4, P4] twice, K2.

Row 3: P1, T3B, [T4F, T4B] twice, T3F, P1.

Row 4: K1, P2, K3, P4, K4, P4, K3, P2, K1.

Row 5: T3B, P3, C4F, P4, C4F, P3, T3F.

Row 6: P2, K4, [P4, K4] twice, P2.

Row 7: K2, P3, T3B, T4F, T4B, T3F, P3, K2.

Row 8: [P2, K3] twice, P4, [K3, P2] twice.

Row 9: [K2, P3] twice, C4B, [P3, K2] twice.

Row 10: As row 8.

Row 11: K2, P3, T3F, T4B, T4F, T3B, P3, K2.

Row 12: As row 6.

Row 13: T3F, P3, C4F, P4, C4F, P3, T3B.

Row 14: As row 4.

Row 15: P1, T3F, [T4B, T4F] twice, T3B, P1.

Row 16: As row 2.

FRONT

Using 4.5mm needles cast on 86 sts.

Foundation row 1 (RS): [P1, K1] 9 times, P2, K9, [P4, K4] 3 times, P4, K9, P2, [K1, P1] 9 times.

Foundation row 2: [P1, K1] 9 times, K2, P9, [K4, P4] 3 times, K4, P9, K2, [K1, P1] 9 times.

Rep foundation rows 1 and 2 once more.

Buttonhole row (RS): [P1, K1] 9 times, P2, K3, cast off next 3 sts (to make a buttonhole, cast on 3 sts over these cast off sts on next row), K2, [P4, K4] 3 times, P4, K3, rep buttonhole over next 3 sts, patt to end.

Rep foundation rows until 12 rows in total have been worked.

Aran pattern placement

(RS) Panel A, P2, Panel B row 1, P2, Panel C row 1, P2, Panel B row 1, P2, Panel A.

(WS) Panel A, K2, Panel B row 2, K2, Panel C row 2, K2, Panel B row 2, K2, Panel A.

Cont with placement as set working 7 full reps of Panel C and 14 full reps of Panel B, work should meas 46cm (18in). With RS facing cast off.

BACK

Using 4.5mm needles cast on 86 sts.

Row 1: P1, ★K1, P1; rep from ★ to end of row.

Rep row 1 until work meas same as Front, cast off.

Press work carefully following instructions on ball band. Sew three sides of cushion cover together leaving edge with buttonholes on open.

I-CORD BUTTONS (make 2)

Using 4.5mm double-pointed needles cast on 6 sts. K6, do not turn work. Push sts to opposite end of needle (leaving yarn at wrong end of work) and pull yarn tightly across back of work, K6. Cont to do this until i-cord is long enough to tie into a knot. Cast off.

Tie i-cord into a knot and sew onto the inside of the back of the cushion cover to correspond with the buttonholes, tucking in the cast-on and cast-off edges to the underside of the knot.

Tie-back version

SIZE
40cm x 40cm (16in x 16in)

YARN
Sirdar Sublime Cashmere Merino Silk Aran (75% extra fine merino, 20% silk, 5% cashmere; 86/50g balls)
Porthole (225) 6 x 50g balls

NEEDLES & ACCESSORIES
1 pair 4.5mm (UK 7/US 7) knitting needles
Cable needle
Cushion pad 40cm x 40cm

SPECIAL ABBREVIATIONS

C2B: Slip 1 st onto cable needle and hold at back of work, K1, K1 from cable needle

C5B: Slip 3 sts onto cable needle and hold at back of work, K2, slip last st from cable needle back onto left-hand needle and P this st, then K2 from cable needle

MB: Make bobble by knitting into next stitch 5 times, turn, P5, turn, K5, turn, P2tog, P1, P2tog, turn, K3tog

T2: Knit into front of 2nd st on left-hand needle, then without slipping this st off K into first st on left-hand needle, slipping both sts off needle at same time

T3B: Slip 1 st onto cable needle and hold at back of work, K2, P1 from cable needle

T3F: Slip 2 sts onto cable needle and hold at front of work, P1, K2 from cable needle

PANEL A

Worked over 20 sts and 2 rows.

Row 1: (RS) [P2, C2B] 5 times.

Row 2: [K2, P2] 5 times.

PANEL B

Worked over 41 sts and 20 rows.

Row 1 (RS): ★T3F, P3, K2, P1, K2, P3, T3B,★ P7; rep from ★ to ★ once.

Row 2: K1, ★P2, K3, P2, K1, P2, K3, P2,★ P9; rep from ★ to ★ once, K1.

Row 3: P1, ★T3F, P2, C5B, P2, T3B,★ P4, MB, P4; rep from ★ to ★ once, P1.

Row 4: K2, ★P2, K2, P2, K1, P2, K2, P2,★ K5, P1, K5; rep from ★ to ★ once, K2.

Row 5: ★P2, [T3F, T3B, P1] twice,★ P2, MB, K3, MB, P1; rep from ★ to ★ once, P1.

Row 6: [K3, P4] twice, K4, P5, K4, [P4, K3] twice.

Row 7: P3, ★K1, T3B, P3, T3F, K1,★ P4, K5, P4; rep from ★ to ★ once, P3.

Row 8: K3, P3, K5, P3, K4, P5, K4, P3, K5, P3, K3.

Row 9: P3, ★T3B, P5, T3F,★ P4, C5B, P4; rep from ★ to ★ once, P3.

Row 10: K3, P2, K7, P2, K4, P2, K1, P2, K4, P2, K7, P2, K3.

Row 11: P2, ★T3B, P7, T3B,★ P3, K2, P1, K2, P3; rep from ★ to ★ once, P2.

Row 12: K2, P2, K9, P2, K3, P2, K1, P2, K3, P2, K9, P2, K2.

Row 13: P1, ★T3B, P4, MB, P4, T3F,★ P2, C5B, P2: rep from ★ to ★ once, P1.

Row 14: K1, P2, K5, P1, K5, P2, K2, P2, K1, P2, K2, P2, K5, P1, K5, P2, K1.

Row 15: ★T3B, P3, MB, K3, MB, P3,★ T3F, T3B, P1, T3F; rep from ★ to ★ once, T3F.

Row 16: P2, K4, P5, K4, P4, K3, P4, K4, P5, K4, P2.

Row 17: K2, P4, K5, P4, K1, T3B, P3, T3F, K1, P4, K5, P4, K2.

Row 18: P2, K4, P5, K4, P3, K5, P3, K4, P5, K4, P2.

Row 19: K2, P4, C5B, P4, T3B, P5, T3F, P4, C5B, P4, K2.

Row 20: ★P2, K4, P2, K1, P2, K4, P2,★ K7; rep from ★ to ★ once.

FRONT

Using 4.5mm needles cast on 85 sts.

Foundation row 1 (RS): [P2, K2] 5 times, P2, ★K2, P4, K2, P1, K2, P4, K2,★ P7; rep from ★ to ★ once, P2, [K2, P2] 5 times.

Foundation row 2: [K2, P2] 5 times, K2, ★P2, K4, P2, K1, P2, K4, P2,★ K7; rep from ★ to ★ once, K2, [P2, K2] 5 times.

Aran pattern placement

(RS): Panel A row 1, P2, Panel B row 1, P2, Panel A row 1.

(WS): Panel A row 2, K2, Panel B row 2, K2, Panel A row 2.

Cont with placement as set working 6 full reps of Panel B. With RS facing cast off.

BACK 1

Using 4.5mm needles cast on 86 sts.

Row 1 (RS): P2, ★C2B, P2; rep from ★ to end of row.

Row 2: K2, ★P2, K2; rep from ★ to end of row.

Rep these 2 rows until work meas 2cm with RS facing for next row.

Next row: Patt 24 sts, [yfwd, K2tog, patt 19 sts] 3 times, patt to end.

Cont straight in patt until work meas 26cm ending with RS facing for next row.

Cast off.

BACK 2

Make as Back 1, omitting lace holes.

Press work carefully following instructions on ball band. Sew cushion cover together overlapping the back pieces, making sure 1 overlaps 2.

I-CORD TIES (make 3)

Using 4.5mm double-pointed needles cast on 3 sts.

K3, do not turn. Push sts to opposite end of needle (leaving yarn at wrong end of work) and pull yarn tightly across back of work, K3. Cont to do this until i-cord is 12cm long, K3tog.

Fold i-cord in half and sew middle point to Back 2 of cushion cover to correspond with lace holes .

Covered button version

PANEL A

Worked over 23 sts and 2 rows.

Row 1 (RS): P.

Row 2: K.

PANEL B

Worked over 6 sts and 16 rows.

Row 1 (RS): P1, MB, P1, T3B.

Row 2: K1, P2, K3.

SIZE
40cm x 40cm (16in x 16in)

YARN
Sirdar Sublime Cashmere Merino Silk Aran (75% extra fine merino, 20% silk, 5% cashmere; 86/50g balls)
Russe (226) 6 x 50g balls

NEEDLES & ACCESSORIES
1 pair 4.5mm (UK 7/US 7) knitting needles
Cable needle
3 x Prym Creative Buttons 22mm (for your nearest stockist, visit www.CoatsCrafts.co.uk)
Cushion pad 40cm x 40cm

SPECIAL ABBREVIATIONS
C4F: Slip 2 sts onto cable needle and hold at front of work, K2, then K2 from cable needle
MB: Make bobble by knitting into next stitch 5 times, turn, P5, turn, K5, turn, P2tog, P1, P2tog, turn, K3tog
T2: K into front of 2nd st on left-hand needle, then without slipping this st off, K into first st on left-hand needle, slipping both sts off needle at same time
T2B: Slip 1 st onto cable needle and hold at back of work, K1, P1 from cable needle
T2F: Slip 1 st onto cable needle and hold at front of work, P1, K1 from cable needle
T3F, T3B, T4B, T4F: See explanations on pages 64 and 65

Row 3: P2, T3B, P1.
Row 4: K2, P2, K2.
Row 5: P1, T3B, P1.
Row 6: K3, P2, K1.
Row 7: T3B, P3.
Row 8: K4, P2.
Row 9: T3F, P1, MB, P1.
Row 10: As row 6.
Row 11: P1, T3F, P2.
Row 12: As row 4.
Row 13: P2, T3F, P1.
Row 14: As row 2.
Row 15: P3, T3F.
Row 16: As row 8.

PANEL C

Worked over 24 sts and 8 rows.
Row 1 (RS): K2, P4, T4F, P1, T2, P1, T4B, P4, K2.
Row 2: P2, K6, [P2, K1] twice, P2, K6, P2.

Row 3: T4F, P4, T4F, T4B, P4, T4B.
Row 4: K2, P2, K6, P4, K6, P2, K2.
Row 5: P2, C4F, P4, T2F, T2B, P4, C4B, P2.
Row 6: K2, P4, K5, P2, K5, P4, K2.
Row 7: T4B, T4F, P3, T2, P3, T4B, T4F.
Row 8: P2, K4, [P2, K3] twice, P2, K4, P2.

FRONT

Using 4.5mm needles cast on 86 sts.
Foundation row 1 (RS): (RS) P27, K2, P2, K2, P4, K4, P1, K2, P1, K4, P4, K2, P2, K2, P27.
Foundation row 2: K27, P2, K2, P2, K4, P4, K1, P2, K1, P4, K4, P2, K2, P2, K27.

Aran pattern placement

(RS) Panel A row 1, P2, Panel B row 1, Panel C row 1, P2, Panel B row 1, P2, Panel A row 1.
(WS) Panel A row 2, K2, Panel B row 2, K2, Panel C row 2, K2, Panel B row 2, K2, Panel A row 2.
Cont with placement as set working 6 full reps of Panel B, 12 of Panel C.
With RS facing cast off.

BACK 1

Using 4.5mm needles cast on 86 sts.
Row 1 (RS): P3 *K3, P3; rep from * to end of row.
Row 2: K3, *P3, K3; rep from * to end of row.
Rep these 2 rows once more ending with RS facing for next row.
Next row: Patt 21 sts, [cast off 3 sts, patt 18 sts] 3 times, patt to end.
Next row: Patt to 3 sts cast off on previous row, cast on 3 sts, rep across row.
Work 2 rows straight then cont in rev st st until work meas 26cm, ending with RS facing for next row.
Cast off.

BACK 2

Make as Back 1, omitting buttonholes.
Press work carefully following instructions on ball band.
Sew cushion cover together overlapping the back pieces, making sure 1 overlaps 2.

COVERED BUTTONS (make 3)

Following the instructions on the packet, darn over Prym Creative Buttons in a design you like. Sew onto Back 2 to correspond with the buttonholes.

5 LIBERATING LACE

A delicate piece of lace that has been knitted in a beautifully fine yarn is a very satisfying project. We particularly love how the patterns reveal themselves as part of the journey. But negotiating all those stitches is often a challenge and when you finish the project your knitting can look a bit underwhelming until you block it. Let our experts help your lace to really bloom.

BLOCKING LACE
Jane Crowfoot

Blocking is the term used to describe the process of washing/wetting, laying out and steaming/drying knitted pieces before they are sewn together. The process evens out the stitches and makes pieces far easier to put together as the seams are less prone to curling.

People block in many different ways, but there are some crucial things to remember and take into consideration. First, if your piece of lace has cast on and cast off edges, make sure this is done loosely. Second, take plenty of time for the 'finishing' process. Never allow a hot iron to touch your knitted fabric. In all cases, avoid placing a hot iron directly onto the knitted fabric as it can cause irreparable damage, especially to synthetic or manmade fibres.

Do not press the ribs, cables and textural stitches. Finally, always read the yarn ball band for washing and finishing instructions.

Blocking lace

Knitting lace can be very time-consuming, especially if you are making a large and beautiful piece which involves working hundreds of stitches and rows in a very fine yarn. The key to really beautiful lace work lies in correct blocking to help it realise its full beauty. The intricate stitching becomes more apparent, the stitches become 'set' in their stretched position and the knitted piece can grow considerably. Having spent so long on a piece, it would be a shame to rush the finish so take your time and adhere to the following steps to ensure the perfect finish.

First steps
Before you start the blocking process, make sure you have the correct equipment.

Blocking board: If you have plenty of room for storage, the ideal surface to work onto is a blocking board. You can make your own board by placing a thin sheet of wadding between a piece of hardboard and some checked or

A few items of specialist equipment make blocking lace much easier.

gingham-type fabric. Stretch the fabric tightly and fix in place with staples or tape. Some people prefer to use a large bathroom towel pinned to the floor, or a blanket covered with a piece of fine cotton fabric such as a bed sheet.

Whatever your preference, bear in mind that the piece needs to be left in place until it is dry, which could take a while.

Mild detergent: The most common outcome of poor care when washing a knitted fabric is felting. This is caused by friction, agitation and heat, or a combination of these.

Different types of yarn require different kinds of care, but the same principles for washing apply to most. Do not use biological washing powder or those with any kind of added brighteners. Soap flakes, mild detergent and specially formulated liquids such as Soak or Eucalan are usually best. If in doubt, test a detergent on a tension swatch before use on the finished item. Make sure the water is cool and the detergent is completely dissolved. If the detergent needs warm or hot water in order to disperse thoroughly, make sure it has had time to cool before washing.

Be careful not to use too much detergent – a small dribble of liquid should suffice.

Clean, thick bath towels: These are used to remove excess water from the knitted fabric. Be careful if using new towels as these can often be 'slippery' and can shed their own fibre.

Pins: Quilters' T-pins are really good for blocking. However, most pins are suitable, but the longer they are, the better. Make sure that the pins you use are rust-proof and easy to handle, and that you have plenty of them!

Blocking wires: Blocking wires are a very handy, if not essential, blocking buddy. You can buy them in packs of four or eight, and they are available in varying lengths. Wires are handy when blocking regular shapes such as squares, triangles and rectangles, but are not used when blocking half or full circles. The use of wires will mean you require fewer pins. You could also try using welding wires, which are available from suppliers such as www.thewelderswarehouse.com, though they may need cleaning before use.

In place of blocking wires, you can opt to use a cotton thread such as a fine yet strong crochet thread. A long length of thread can be sewn through the perimeter stitches of the knitted lace, leaving a loop at each corner.

Place a pin into each corner loop and arrange the knitting along the taut string, pinning in pairs as you go.

Metre rule or set square: A ruler of some kind will help you to ensure that you have blocked your piece straight and evenly.

Washing

Always wash one piece at a time. Do not wring, twist or rub the fabric, and never use a brush to remove spots or stains. You will need to leave the piece to soak for a minimum of 15 minutes to ensure that the yarn has absorbed its optimum amount of water **(1)**. Some yarns (cotton and linen especially) can take surprisingly long to soak fully. Always make sure the water runs clear after the final rinse.

Remove as much water as you can by pushing the knitted piece gently against the side of the basin or bowl in which you have washed it.

When you've managed to remove a fair amount of water, you will need to transfer the piece onto a clean towel. It is vital that you support the piece in its transition from basin to towel. By placing the piece in a colander, you will support the fabric fully and avoid excess stretching and pulling.

Flatten your knitted piece between two clean, thick bath towels and carefully press to remove excess water. You need to remove as much water as possible in this

process. Some people roll the knitting up in the towel and push against it. Others lay the piece out flat between the two towels and carefully walk on it or add weight of some kind.

Pinning out

Gently pin your knitted piece onto your chosen blocking surface.

2   For a geometric shape such as a triangle, square or rectangle, pin out the corners first, followed by the top middle point then the corresponding point opposite this on the bottom edge, stretching the piece slightly in order to achieve its true length.

3   Always place the pins in pairs from the centre out, making sure that for every pin you place you also put in its 'partner' along the opposite edge.

4   This will ensure that you pin out evenly. Use your ruler to ensure that you are pinning in a straight line (this is where a gingham or checked blocking board cover comes in handy, as you can pin along the fabric lines).

5   For geometric shapes you can replace some of the pins with blocking wires. These are carefully threaded through the edge stitches of the knitted fabric. Use your fingers to ease along the edges so that the lace is fully stretched out. Place pins at each corner and at a couple of places along the edges to secure the lace.

6+7   For a circular shape, pin out the four compass points, then work around the piece, placing pins in pairs as for a geometric shape.

8   To ensure a true circle you may want to work on top of an image. To do this, draw a circle using a fine pencil or dressmaker's chalk onto the blocking board and pin out to the drawn line.

Let it dry

The impatient among you will have to take yourself out for the day or settle down to knit your next project in front of a few good movies before the piece is dry. Do not be tempted to unpin your piece until you are convinced it is thoroughly dry. You may find that the piece has raised itself away from the blocking board slightly and has gone pretty taut – a little like the skin of a drum. This is caused by the yarn retracting as it dries. The drying time will depend on the climate, but the general rule of thumb is to wait 24 hours. Just remember that the wait is worth it! The blocking process will need to be repeated every time the lace piece is washed.

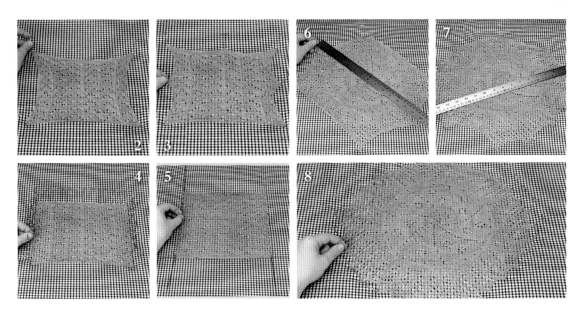

CREATING PERFECT LACE
Jane Crowfoot

The complexity and labour-intensive nature of lace patterns mean it's all too easy to make mistakes, and this can be off-putting to those embarking upon their first lace project. However, there are some really useful tips that can help you to produce that elusive piece of perfect lace.

Here you will find some easy ways to avoid making mistakes in the first place, then explore the techniques you can use should the worst happen.

If you're new to lace knitting, we'd recommend starting with a small project that has lace patterning on alternate rows. This type of project is referred to as lace knitting, as opposed to knitted lace which has lace patterning on all rows.

Helpful equipment

Here's our list of tools for lace knitters:
Safety pins: Of various sizes, these are fantastic for grabbing that dropped stitch as soon as you spot it.
Waste yarn: Used to make stitch and row markers, to hold live stitches and also to make 'life-lines'. It is best if it is smooth and finer than the knitting yarn – crochet cotton is our favourite. Make sure it is colourfast so that you can wash it with your lace, if necessary, and certainly check that the dye won't rub off onto your work.
Pencil: Very helpful to mark any notes on the chart straight away before you forget. We don't use pen just in case we get ink on our fingers and then on our knitting.
Contrast background: A piece of fabric or card. If you need to sort out a mistake, you can use it as a background to help the stitches to show up really clearly.
Tapestry needle: As fine as possible.
Crochet hook: Same gauge as the knitting needles or finer, for picking up stitches.
Double-pointed needles: Again, the same gauge as the knitting needles or finer, used for working up several stitches at a time.

Choosing the right pattern and yarn

When choosing your first lace pattern, look for a project that will enable you to try different stitches without being too overwhelming. It's also worth trying to avoid yarns that are hard to unravel, and dark-coloured yarns which can make the stitches hard to see.

Reading charts

The majority of lace patterns are now presented in chart form, particularly more complex patterns. Each instruction

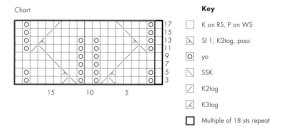

Chart

Key

☐ K on RS, P on WS
⋌ Sl 1, K2tog, psso
O yo
⟍ SSK
⟋ K2tog
⋋ K3tog
☐ Multiple of 18 sts repeat

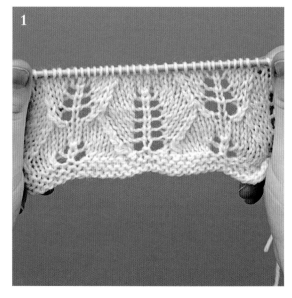

1

is represented by a symbol within the chart. These symbols are designed to show how they look in the knitted fabric.

Yarnovers, for example, will appear as holes in the knitted fabric and are shown as circles on a chart. Right-leaning decreases (K2tog on RS) are shown as right-leaning slashes.

Compare the central section of the sample below left **(1)** with its chart to see how the two relate to each other. Because this sample is lace knitting, the chart shows only RS rows; all WS rows are purled.

Tips and suggestions

It is worth charting written instructions if a chart is not provided. This will build a picture of what the pattern repeat should look like, and makes it much easier to spot mistakes. Alternatively, you can use the tension swatch as a reference. If your project has any shaping, make copies of the chart and draw the increases or decreases on it to help you decide how to handle those edge stitches.

Always work in good light. Natural light is best, but the modern range of daylight bulbs makes for an excellent substitute.

Always have a towel over your lap which shows up the pattern of the work well and protects both you and the knitting from dye or fibre transfer.

Keep track of your place in the pattern repeat either on the written instructions or the chart. Sticky notes, a ruler or magnetic strips all have their purpose here.

Quite apart from checking your tension, which is usually not so critical here, use the tension swatch to familiarise yourself with the pattern and the yarn.

Put a stitch marker either side of each repeat if it is large or several repeats if it is only a few stitches. If you have made a mistake which has thrown the row out, you can locate it quickly by checking the number of stitches between the markers. It is particularly useful to mark the repeat at the end of the row where there is shaping; if increasing, mark the last one, and once sufficient stitches have been added to allow the next full repeat, mark it. If decreasing, mark at least the last two, more if necessary, to make sure there is always at least one full repeat marked at the end of each row. Often the pattern needs to be fudged somewhat until a full repeat is restored and so the markers are an important point of reference both to check the number of increases or decreases made and to keep the pattern correct.

Avoiding mistakes

It is common to make mistakes when working early repeats of a lace pattern. Once you have done a few repeats, the pattern will become easier to memorise, and you'll be able to recognise where you are. However, taking a few preventative measures can save lots of time.

Chart copy, sticky notes and markers

You can make a working copy of the chart, for your own personal use. Enlarging it will make it easier to read, and you can keep notes on the back of it as well.

Sticky notes are a really great way of keeping track of where you are in your pattern. Use them to block out the rows above or below, so you can see how the row you are working lines up with your knitting.

Stitch markers are useful when placed after each repeat of the stitch pattern in the row, to help you keep track of where you are in the pattern. Purpose-made markers are available, or you could simply use a knotted loop of mercerised cotton yarn.

Using a life-line

A life-line is a piece of yarn threaded through a knitted row at the end of the pattern repeat. If a mistake is subsequently made, then the knitting can be unravelled back to the life-line and no further.

Life-lines can be used after each pattern repeat, or at the halfway point. In really complicated lace patterns, you may want to insert a life-line every couple of rows.

1   Use a large sewing needle with a blunt point and a smooth contrasting thread. Make sure the thread is long enough to leave you with ample yarn once sewn through the row. Mercerised cotton is perfect because it won't stick to the working yarn.

2   Sew through the centre of each stitch on the knitting needle, being careful not to sew through any stitch markers. If there isn't enough space to do this on the needle, slip the stitches off onto the sewing thread, and then slide the needle back in, once all stitches are on the life-line.

3   Make sure that the life-line thread cannot loosen or unravel itself from the row. Perhaps use safety pins to secure it at each tail end, or tie the ends in a knot.

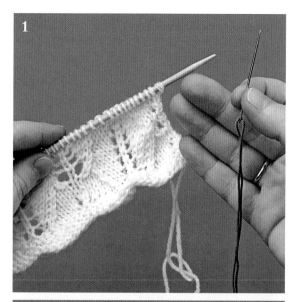

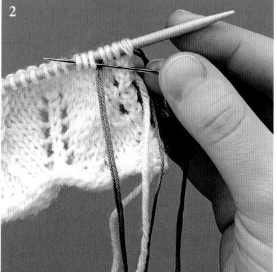

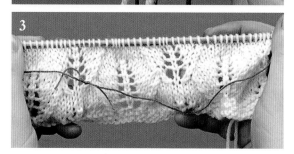

CORRECTING MISTAKES IN LACE
Judy Furlong

There are few things more stomach-churning than dropping a stitch or spotting an error in a particularly impressive bit of lace knitting. Many a knotted sample has been relegated to the bottom of the knitting bag as a result. It's enough to put some knitters off lace for life.

The easiest way to fix a mistake is to avoid it in the first place. Here are some 'Golden Rules': suggestions to make life a little easier and a lot less stressful!

How to spot mistakes early

Do keep checking for mistakes. If you have a huge number of stitches on the needle – far too many to stretch them all out – check a section at a time, work a little further along the row then look at the next bit, and so on until you are happy with the whole row. It might be worth moving onto a circular needle to spread out the stitches.

When correcting lace mistakes you will sometimes be unpicking sections of stitches within a row, or sometimes an entire row. You may notice that the yarn you have unpicked is kinked, and does not re-knit in exactly the same way, making it appear different from the rest of your lace. However, when you come to dress or block your lace, you should find that these noticeable differences melt away.

If you are really concerned about the quality of the re-knitted yarn, you may wish to consider using new yarn in its place. It can be tricky to add yarn in the middle of a row, so on the following pages we give an overview of the different ways you can achieve this. Laceweight yarns can be fairly fragile and so watch out for anything which might snag your work, and be especially careful around rings and some stitch markers.

Avoid bunching – if there are lots of stitches, think about using a circular needle which will accommodate them better. It is easy to drop stitches when moving them along the needle, particularly if you tend towards tight tension – that little tug might just pull them off the end.

Finally, dressing or blocking – be vigilant when stretching out your lace, just in case there is a missed dropped stitch, and stand by with those safety pins!

It helps to note that a great many lace pattern stitches are symmetrical. Having worked through the pattern a few times, you will have started to take note of a few pointers;

for example, a central knit stitch and central yarn overs either side. If you spot that these key stitches are out, find the mistake by looking at the stitch count between the markers or, failing that, start at the beginning of the row you are on and check what you have actually worked and be particularly alert for missed yarn overs.

Mark the place with waste yarn using a fine crochet hook to insert it **(1)**, but if it is a dropped stitch, grab it first with a safety pin to prevent it unravelling – no need for the waste yarn as the pin will mark the place **(2)**.

If the whole row from that point is wrong, unpick stitch by stitch, back to the first mistake. Otherwise, if it was just a dropped stitch for example and the rest of the row is fine, mark the place and correct it on the next row.

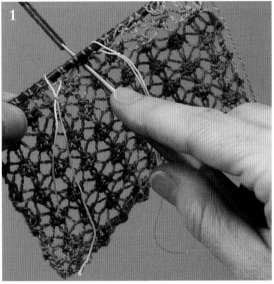

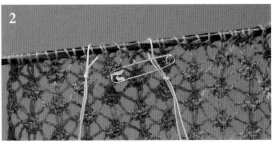

Unpicking stitch by stitch

The aim is to catch the stitches of the row below on the RH needle, working one stitch at a time to the place where the first mistake happened. It can help to refer to the pattern (remembering to read the row below, of course!) so you are warned when a particularly awkward stitch, like a central decrease, is coming up.

Turn the work so that the mistake is on the LH needle.

1   Holding the yarn fairly taut in the RH, unpick stitch by stitch, by inserting the tip of the RH needle into the stitch below the first on the LH needle and lift it off. Gently pull the yarn from that stitch, now safely on the RH needle.

2   Keep going until you reach the marker and be particularly careful when handling yarn overs.

Now all that remains is to fix the problem. Usually the tension is a little different from the neighbouring stitches and might need a little tweaking to restore things to perfection.

Unpicking whole rows

Sometimes the problem is a lot more extensive than just an odd mistake or two, and really the easiest – and in the long run, quickest – solution can be to take the work back to a recognisable row. Some stitch patterns make this easy by having several rows of garter stitch in each repeat.

Lay out the work as flat as possible and identify the first of the knit rows, or at least one which has predominantly knit or purl stitches.

1   Follow the position of the markers down to this row and put them in here using a crochet hook. Gently pull the stitches off the needle and slowly unravel the knitting down to the row above the selected row, winding up the yarn as you go. Don't tug at anything, but gently ease out any knots – cut the yarn if necessary, but don't just pull, as some stitches might unravel too far.

2   Using a needle, preferably finer than the one which is being used for the knitting, pick up the stitches starting from the free yarn end, unpicking the previous row as you go – just as for unpicking stitch by stitch, remembering to slip the new markers onto the needle.

Check this row against the pattern to ensure nothing has been missed. Be really careful when working it, checking none of the stitches has been dropped or twisted.

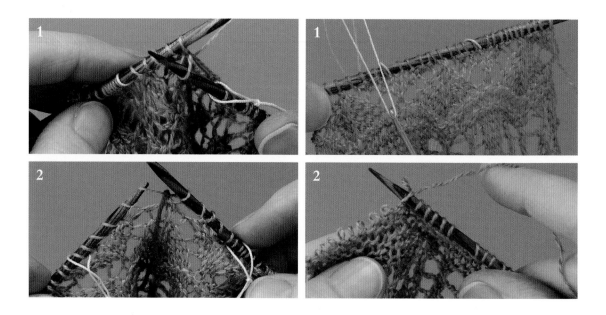

Unpicking just one repeat

You don't always have to unpick entire rows when you've made a mistake.

1   You can drop as few or as many stitches as you like, even up to the whole repeat where the mistake happened, unravelling them right down to the life-line. The markers will help you identify whereabouts in the repeat you are. Note the loose threads – one for each row that was unpicked.

2   Slip the stitches onto a double-pointed needle and check that the row is correct according to the pattern.

3+4   Using a crochet hook and double-pointed needles, work the stitches back up using the appropriate thread for that row until all the rows have been worked.

Fixing missed yarn overs

A very common mistake is to forget to work a yarn over. This can throw the whole row out by one stitch from that point so it is fairly easy to spot.

Unpick stitch by stitch to that point. Insert the LH needle under the yarn lying between the two stitches and there – you have your yarn over. It will be a little tighter than it ought to be, but that can be evened out at the end, when blocking.

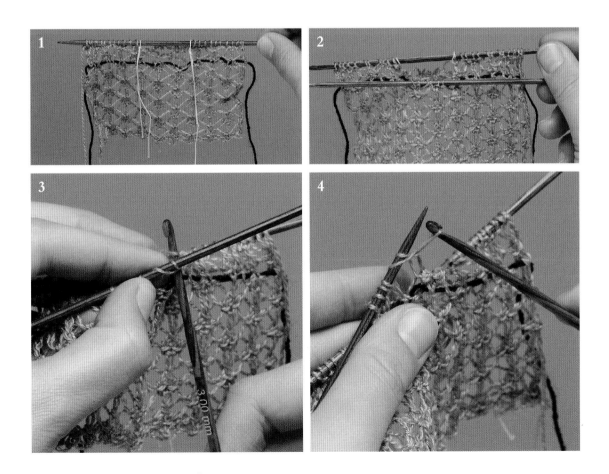

Fixing dropped yarn overs

If a stitch is dropped which was worked on a yarn over on the previous row, it just leaves two pretty loose looking threads without a stitch in sight!

Turn the work so that the knit side of the dropped stitch is facing.

1   Insert the tip of the RH needle (or a crochet hook), below the bottom thread (this was the 'yarn over') from front to back.

2   Bring the tip up and forwards between the two strands and catch the thread above, pushing it backwards and down.

3   Bring it under the bottom thread, forwards and upwards (this is the dropped stitch).

4   Slip it onto the LH needle.

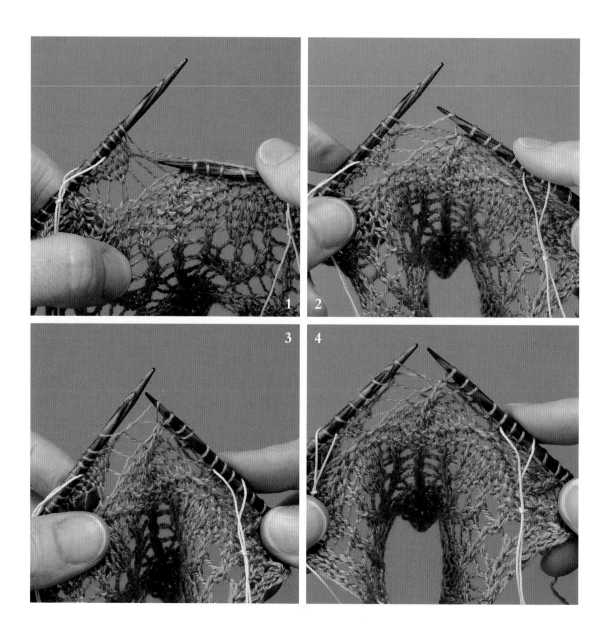

Picking up dropped decreases

There will be a little cluster of stitches, hopefully already spotted and sitting on a safety pin.

1 Transfer them (or pick them up) onto a double-pointed needle. Note the loose yarn above from which these stitches unravelled. Check what sort of decrease it should have been to make sure the slope is correct – for example, K2tog slopes rightwards, SSK leftwards, cdd (central double decrease) is central and it is this last one in the illustration.

Work the decrease as instructed – for this we usually use a crochet hook. Using cdd for this example, insert the hook into the second, then the first, then the third stitch.

2 Pick up the loose thread above and pull it through the last stitch onto the crochet hook. With the tip of the double-pointed needle or crochet hook, slip the first 2 stitches over the knitted one.

3 Replace the mended stitch onto the left-hand needle.

If the final stitch looks a lot looser than you expected, check the pattern to make sure there were no yarn overs either side, in which case just pick up the yarn either side of the stitch.

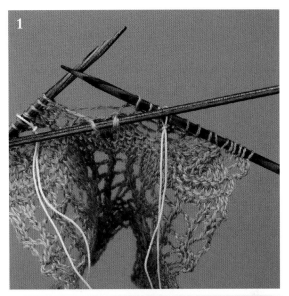

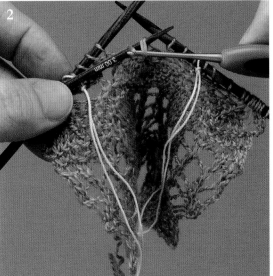

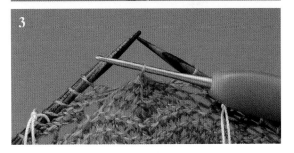

Joining yarn

If yarn needs to be joined, either because the ball ran out,
the yarn broke or there was a knot, whatever the reason it
is not always appropriate or desirable to join yarn at the
end of a row. This is especially so if the garment is a scarf
with the row end being a selvedge.

There are many ways to join within a row, such as
unwinding and then twisting the yarns together **(1+2)**, and
splicing **(3+4)**, but my current favourite is the Russian
join.

Russian join

1–3   Thread a tapestry needle with the end of the yarn and manoeuvre the needle through the centre of the same piece of yarn, making a loop.

4+5   Put the end of the new yarn through the loop, thread it into a tapestry needle and manoeuvre it through itself as for the first yarn end.

6   Gently pull on the ends to tighten the join. Continue knitting, taking care to leave the ends free.

However, this is no use if the yarn is a single ply.

7   When working with cobweb-weight yarn, simply select the finest part of both ends, twist them together and work with double thickness for a few stitches, choosing the least 'open' part of the lace.

This is especially useful for disguising joins and weaving in loose ends in solid areas such as nupps or bobbles.
   Whatever the method, trim the ends to a few centimetres but never flush to the lace until after dressing, just in case they pull out.

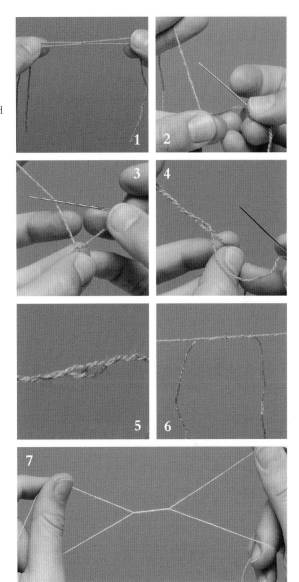

Take heart

If, even after all this care, you spot a mistake when you've finished knitting the whole piece, console yourself that it can't be that obvious or you would have noticed it earlier.

   Although we would all like everything to be absolutely perfect, don't be put off. Slight imperfections are part of the charm of handwork, otherwise we might as well make everything by machine. It probably won't be the last piece of lace you knit, and just think how much your project has taught you. Good luck, and above all, have fun!

GOLDEN WHEAT LACE SHAWL
Jen Arnall-Culliford

This heirloom piece features beautiful lace patterning and a stunning custom-dyed yarn.

Knitwear designs often start out as an idea in one person's head, and are then brought to life by a team effort. That's what happened with Jen Arnall-Culliford's gorgeous Golden Wheat Lace Shawl.

Says Jen: 'My inspiration came from *Knitted Lace of Estonia* by Nancy Bush – I saw how nupps could be used to make wheat-like motifs. I played around with stitch patterns, combining ideas from a number of sources, before settling on the three main areas: centre, border and edging.

'The centre of the shawl is worked back and forth on straight needles before being joined in the round. The shawl is then worked from the middle outwards in a central lace pattern followed by a border pattern. Finally a knitted-on edging is used to cast off all stitches.'

Working full-time as *The Knitter* magazine's technical editor, Jen simply didn't have time to realise the ideas in her head herself, so expert sample knitter Kim Hobley did the creating. The third team member was the talented Lilith at Old Maiden Aunt Yarns. "Lilith custom-dyed the alpaca merino silk laceweight yarn to the shade of golden wheat and did a wonderful job," says Jen.

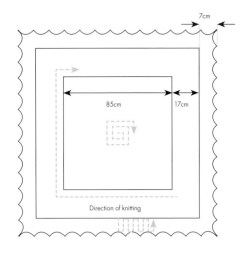

7cm

85cm   17cm

Direction of knitting

Pattern notes

You may find it helpful to use one set of stitch markers to mark the end of each side of the shawl (corner), and another set to mark each pattern repeat within the sides. When working the plain rows of the central lace pattern (knit or purl depending on whether you are working flat or in the round), you will need to work through the back loop of the second yarn over from the previous row. To make the nupps easier to work, make sure that the 5st inc is worked very loosely, making the 5tog decrease much easier. Using a needle with a long tapered point will also help. If you still struggle, then try pulling the loop through on the decrease with a much thinner needle and slipping the stitch onto your normal needle, or work using a crochet hook.

Stitch patterns

Central lace pattern

Starts with 24 sts (6 on each side). Also shown on chart.
Row 1: ★K1, yo, K2tog, yo twice, SSK, yo, K1; rep from ★ to end of row. 32 sts.
Row 2 and all foll even-numbered rows: Purl all sts, working through back loop of second yarn over of previous row if needed.
Row 3: ★K1, yo, K2tog, yo, K2, yo, SSK, yo, K1; rep from ★ to end of row. 40 sts.
Row 5: ★KFB, yo, K2tog, yo, K4, yo, SSK, yo, KFB; rep from ★ to end of row. 56 sts.
Row 7: ★KFB, yo, K3tog, yo, K1, yo, K4, yo, K1, yo, SSSK, yo, KFB; rep from ★ to end of row. 72 sts.
Row 9: ★K1, yo, K2tog, yo twice, SSK, K2, yo, SSK, K2tog, yo, K2, K2tog, yo twice, SSK, yo, K1; rep from ★ to end of row. 80 sts.
Row 11: ★K1, yo, K2tog, yo, K2, yo, SSK, K6, K2tog, yo, K2, yo, SSK, yo, K1; rep from ★ to end of row. 88 sts.
Row 13: ★KFB, yo, K2tog, yo, K4, yo, SSK, K4, K2tog, yo, K4, yo, SSK, yo, KFB; rep from ★ to end of row. 104 sts.
Row 15: ★KFB, yo, K3tog, yo, K1, yo, K4, yo, K1, yo, SSSK, K3tog, K1, yo, K4, yo, K1, yo, SSSK, yo, KFB; rep from ★ to end of row. 120 sts.
Rnd 17: ★★K1, yo, K2tog, yo twice, SSK, K2, yo, SSK, ★K2tog, yo, K2, K2tog, yo twice, SSK, K2, yo, SSK; rep from ★ to last 9 sts of side, K2tog, yo, K2, K2tog, yo twice, SSK, yo, K1. Rep from ★★ 3 more times.
Rnd 18 and all foll even-numbered rnds: Knit all sts, working through the back loop of second yarn over of previous row if needed.
Rnd 19: ★★K1, yo, K2tog, yo, K2, yo, SSK, K3, ★K3, K2tog, yo, K2, yo, SSK, K3; rep from ★ to last 10 sts of side, K3, K2tog, yo, K2, yo, SSK, yo, K1. Rep from ★★ 3 more times.
Rnd 21: ★★KFB, yo, K2tog, yo, K4, yo, SSK, K2, ★K2, K2tog, yo, K4, yo, SSK, K2; rep from ★ to last 11 sts of side, K2, K2tog, yo, K4, yo, SSK, yo, KFB. Rep from ★★ 3 more times.
Rnd 23: ★★KFB, yo, K3tog, yo, K1, yo, K4, yo, K1, yo, SSSK, ★K3tog, yo, K1, yo, K4, yo, K1, yo, SSSK; rep from ★ to last 13 sts of side, K3tog, yo, K1, yo, K4, yo, K1, yo, SSSK, yo, KFB. Rep from ★★ 3 more times.
Last 8 rounds form centre lace panel repeat.

Shawl

Centre panel

Using 2.75mm straight needles cast on 8 sts.

Next row (RS): KFB 8 times. 16 sts.

Next row: *PFB, P2, PFB; rep from * to end. 24 sts.

Row 1: Work from Chart A or written instructions, repeating the marked section 4 times. 32 sts.

Row 2: Purl all sts, working through back loop of second yarn over of previous row.

Work from chart, or written stitch pattern, until row 15 is completed, working all even rows as row 2 given above. 120 sts.

Row 16 (WS): Purl all sts onto a set of 2.75mm DPNs (or circular needles using the 'Magic Loop' method). Turn and join to work in the round. From this point until the end of the border, the shawl is worked in the round, so all rows are RS rows.

Rnds 17–24: Work from chart or written instructions above, working across all four sides of square in each round. Even-numbered rounds are knitted, with the second yarn over from previous round knitted through the back loop where necessary. 168 sts.

Rnds 25–32: Work from chart or written instructions, repeating marked section twice on each side of square. 216 sts.

Rnds 33–40: Work from chart or written instructions, repeating marked section 3 times on each side of square. 264 sts.

Cont to work as set, and once each 8-row section is complete, check your stitch count has increased by 48 sts (see end of round totals below). These extra stitches correspond to 12 sts per side and are worked as an extra repeat of the marked section.

Continue to work from chart or written instructions until round 152 is complete. Round 152 will have the marked section repeated 17 times on each side of square. 936 sts (234 sts on each side of square.)

Rnd 48: 312 sts.

Rnd 64: 408 sts.

Rnd 80: 504 sts.

Rnd 96: 600 sts.

Rnd 112: 696 sts.

Rnd 128: 792 sts.

Rnd 144: 888 sts.

Rnd 152: 936 sts. (234 sts on each side of square.)

Border

Next rnd: *P1, yo, purl to last st before end of side, yo, P1; rep from * 3 more times. 944 sts.

Next rnd: Knit.

Rep last 2 rounds 3 more times. 968 sts. (242 sts per side.)

Rnd 1: Work from Chart B, repeating marked 40st repeat 6 times on each side of square, and each whole row of chart 4 times in each round. 976 sts.

Rnds 2–72: Work from chart as set above. See notes above for help working nupps. 1256 sts. (314 sts on each side.)

Edging

Next rnd: K157 to take you to the middle of one side of the square.

Use a provisional cast on method to cast 13 sts onto a 2.75mm DPN.

Work from Chart C or written instructions below, with WS of main shawl facing you, to effectively cast off the shawl stitches by working this edging.

Row 1 (RS): Sl 1, (yo, K2tog) twice, P1, 5-st nupp, yo, K1, yo, 5-st nupp, K2, K2tog.

Row 2: P3, P5tog, P3, P5tog, K1, (yo, K2tog) twice, P2togE. 14 edging sts.

Row 3: Sl 1, (yo, K2tog) twice, P1, K1, 5-st nupp, yo, K1, yo, 5-st nupp, K2, K2tog.

Row 4: P3, P5tog, P3, P5tog, P1, K1, (yo, K2tog) twice, P2togE. 15 edging sts.

Row 5: Sl 1, (yo, K2tog) twice, P1, K2, 5-st nupp, yo, K1, yo, 5-st nupp, K2, K2tog.

Row 6: P3, P5tog, P3, P5tog, P2, K1, (yo, K2tog) twice, P2togE. 16 edging sts.

Row 7: Sl 1, (yo, K2tog) twice, P1, K3, 5-st nupp, yo, K1, yo, 5-st nupp, K2, K2tog.

Row 8: P3, P5tog, P3, P5tog, P3, K1, (yo, K2tog) twice, P2togE. 17 edging sts.

Row 9: Sl 1, (yo, K2tog) twice, P1, K4, 5-st nupp, yo, K1, yo, 5-st nupp, K2, K2tog.

Row 10: P3, P5tog, P3, P5tog, P4, K1, (yo, K2tog) twice, P2togE. 18 edging sts.

Row 11: Sl 1, (yo, K2tog) twice, P1, K5, 5-st nupp, yo, K1, yo, 5-st nupp, K2, K2tog.

Row 12: P3, P5tog, P3, P5tog, P5, K1, (yo, K2tog) twice, P2togE. 19 edging sts.

Row 13: Sl 1, (yo, K2tog) twice, P1, K6, 5-st nupp, yo, K1, yo, 5-st nupp, K2, K2tog.

Row 14: P3, P5tog, P3, P5tog, P6, K1, (yo, K2tog) twice, P2togE. 20 edging sts.

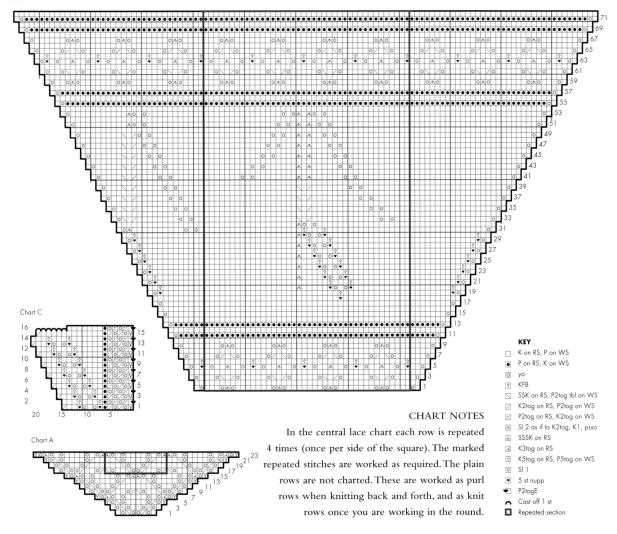

Chart B

Chart C

Chart A

KEY

KEY

□	K on RS, P on WS
⊡	P on RS, K on WS
○	yo
Ⅴ	KFB
⟍	SSK on RS, P2tog tbl on WS
⟋	K2tog on RS, P2tog on WS
⟍	P2tog on RS, K2tog on WS
⋀	Sl 2 as if to K2tog, K1, psso
⋀	SSSK on RS
⟋	K3tog on RS
⟋	K5tog on RS, P5tog on WS
Ⅴ	Sl 1
♥	5 st nupp
♥	P2togE
⌒	Cast off 1 st
▣	Repeated section

CHART NOTES

In the central lace chart each row is repeated 4 times (once per side of the square). The marked repeated stitches are worked as required. The plain rows are not charted. These are worked as purl rows when knitting back and forth, and as knit rows once you are working in the round.

Row 15: Sl 1, (yo, K2tog) twice, P1, K12, K2tog. 19 edging sts.
Row 16: Cast off 6 sts, purl to 7 sts on RH needle, K1, (yo, K2tog) twice, P2togE. 13 edging sts.
Work these 16 rows 19 times in total. 5 sts should remain on main shawl border before corner.

Turn corner of shawl

Work rows 1–16 of edging as follows twice, to turn corner on shawl, and take you to 5 sts past the corner.
On rows 2, 8 and 14, leave border stitch on needle, having worked P2togE. This means that two joins will be worked into the same border stitch on these rows. All other rows are worked as written above.

Work rows 1–16 of edging as written, 38 times. This should take you to 5 sts before next corner. Work corner as above.

Repeat on remaining sides, finishing with 19 repeats of edging to join start of edging.

Undo provisional cast-on and graft 13 sts from each end together.

Making up

Sew short seam together at centre.
Weave in all ends, but don't trim.
Block shawl to measurements. Allow shawl to dry thoroughly and trim any ends.

6 FAIR ISLE TECHNIQUES

Here, we explore the different techniques of knitting Fair Isle as well as how to re-colour patterns. Discover your ideal Fair Isle technique and you'll produce perfect knits every time.

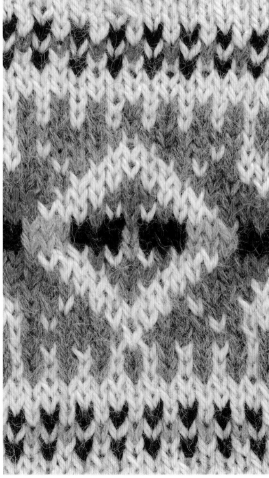

FLAWLESS FAIR ISLE
Jane Crowfoot

The knitting term Fair Isle is used to describe the process of working two or more continuous yarns across a row of knitted fabric to create a repeated (often geometric and small-scale) pattern. A traditional Fair Isle pattern uses just two colours per row and has a small number of stitches between each colour change, although Fair Isle designs can use more than two colours and have larger areas of one colour between changes.

The most common problem people have when working a Fair Isle design is from twisted threads, which can lead to knots in the knitting yarn and inconsistent weaving where strands of yarn are carried across the reverse of the work. This can lead to an uneven tension and baggy stitches.

Holding your needles

We all hold our knitting needles and perform the process of knitting in different ways (see page 154). Some of us hold our needles rather like we would our knife and fork; others hold the right needle as if it were a pencil. Some of us hold the yarn in our left hand and work the Continental style, while some knit with the yarn in the right hand. Whichever way you choose to knit, there's a Fair Isle technique suited to you. Below you'll find three ways of holding the yarn and needles. Practise all three and decide which is best for you.

Using the right hand to work two yarns

In the Shetland Isles, the most common way of holding the yarns is with both in the right hand. This takes a bit of practice because it involves using the middle finger as well as the index finger. Our middle fingers are seldom used, so tend to be a little lazy – you may find that this method makes it ache a little at first.

At the beginning of the row, determine which yarn is to be used the most. Wrap this yarn around your right index finger, allowing the yarn to hang down inside the palm of your hand. Take the contrast colour, which is to be used less frequently, around your middle finger and allow it to hang down inside the palm of your hand alongside the predominant colour.

To work the stitches in the correct colour sequence, bring either the index finger or the middle finger into position and wrap the yarn around the needle in the usual way to complete the knitted stitch.

It's common for the tension of the yarn to be difficult to control because one yarn tends to sag while the other is in use. The more you practise, the easier it will become to control this tension.

To make it easier – and to add a bit of weight to the yarn end which will make it less likely to sag – you may choose to wrap the yarn around a bobbin and keep the yarn close to the knitted fabric you're working.

Working two yarns from the same hand means that one is automatically carried over the top of the other, so there's no likelihood of the yarns becoming twisted.

Using the left hand to work two yarns

This is the method used by Continental knitters. Both yarns are held in the left hand and wrapped around the left index finger from front to back.

In order to knit a stitch in the correct colour, use the right knitting needle to 'pick' the yarn to be used from the left hand. This is rather like a crochet action because it's the needle and not the yarn that needs to be manipulated in order to complete the stitch.

Both yarns sit behind the two knitting needles. In order to knit a stitch, wrap the right knitting needle around the chosen yarn, so that the yarn leads from back to front in an anticlockwise direction, and draw it through the original stitch.

Using both hands to work two yarns

Hold the predominant yarn in your right hand in your usual manner. Hold the contrast yarn in the left hand, in a mirror image of the yarn held in the right hand **(1, on page 88)**. The tension of the yarn can be difficult to control if you aren't used to holding things in your left hand. This will come with practice.

When knitting the predominant colour, knit in the usual way, wrapping the yarn around the knitting needle using the right hand.

In order to knit a stitch in the contrast colour, use the right knitting needle to 'pick' the yarn to be used from the left hand. Again, this is rather like a crochet action – the yarn is wrapped around the needle in an anticlockwise direction and drawn through the original stitch.

The importance of consistent stranding and weaving

As you work along the row, you'll notice that the yarn not in use between the small blocks of colour automatically becomes stranded across the back of the work, creating a 'float'.

It's important that the floats are carried in a consistent manner (2) so that the yarns don't become twisted and the tension of the knitted pieces is kept regular. (The swatch in picture 3 shows inconsistent stranding.)

By working any of the above methods and working in the round on either circular needles or sets of DPNs, the yarns shouldn't become twisted because neither is wrapped around the other at any time. If you aren't working in the round then you'll need to be aware of the yarns twisting when changing from a right-side row to a wrong-side row. If you do notice a cross-over in the yarn, reposition the yarns to unravel the twist.

Dealing with yarn ends and joining a new yarn

Take the time to tidy things up as you work. Being disciplined about this will help you in the long run, and will mean you don't end up with the nasty job of dealing with all the yarn ends once your knitting is complete.

Towards the end of your knitting session, make sure you allow enough time to tidy things up. This way, when you next pick up your knitting it will be neat and tidy and ready for action. Wherever possible, weave in a yarn end as you work.

Always have in mind what colour changes will take place in the future. If you're nearing the end of the use of one colour, have a look at your pattern to see which colour needs to be joined next and weave this in while working the last few stitches of the current row. This way, the new yarn will be joined and ready to start the new row when you need it (4+5).

'Invisible' changes

These two methods of changing yarn completely eliminate yarn ends and are great if you're feeling thrifty!

Splicing

This is a method of joining a new yarn that our grandmothers' generation was very familiar with. It can be a little unreliable because it weakens the yarn and is only really completely dependable when used with pure wool, although hairy yarns such as alpaca and mohair are also pretty good for this method.

Unravel the yarn plies for approximately 5cm, so that they open out, making sure you have approximately half the number of plies in both yarns.

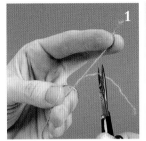 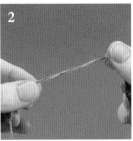

1   Using a sharp pair of scissors, trim half the ends on each piece of yarn to half the length.

2   Twist one long ply from one yarn together with a short end from the other in order to mimic the original twist of the yarn. Twist the remaining plies in the same way.

3   Once you've twisted the yarns together, moisten the yarn using a little warm (but not hot) water and then rub the yarns together in the palm of your hand. The friction and heat created will felt the yarns together and reinforce the join.

Russian join

This is another nifty method of invisibly joining a new yarn. See the step-by-step instructions in chapter 5 on pages 80–81.

Dominance

When two yarns are held consistently, the yarn held below will have slightly longer stitches. This means that this shade will be more dominant in the finished knitted item. If you hold the motif shade below the background shade, the motif will stand out more than if you hold the yarns the other way round. The key is consistency, and even the WS looks neat when the yarns are held the same way throughout (4).

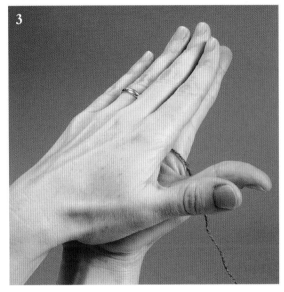

RE-COLOURING FAIR ISLE DESIGNS
Emma King

As knitters, we all get excited about colour. We are very lucky with regards to colours available to us – we have huge yarn ranges to choose from, thanks to the introduction of artificial dyes. In fact, we have so many to choose from that when we have to make our own colour decisions we can find ourselves struggling to make the correct choice! An area that can be particularly daunting is Fair Isle, and so here we are going to look at how you would set about re-colouring a Fair Isle design.

A colourful history

We associate Fair Isle with colour. Fair Isle knitting uses two or more colours and relies on a balanced palette to make it successful. However, Fair Isle was once quite lacking in colour – early Fair Isle garments created on the Shetland Isles saw the islanders relying on the natural white, grey and brown yarns produced by the local breeds for their designs. This 'lack' of colour didn't in any way hinder the impact of the designs – these natural shades still provided stunning results due to how the knitters selected and used them. The more colourful Fair Isles that we see

today are still only successful if the colours are selected and used in the right way, and it's this that we want to focus on.

The chart below **(2)** shows a design in its original colour palette which we will be using as our reference point. The chart is also shown in its comparative shades of grey, as though the colour version has been photocopied, to show the tonal values of the colours **(1)**.

There are various reasons as to why you might want to re-colour a Fair Isle – the yarns that the designer has used might not be available anymore, or perhaps you love the design but the colours used are not the sort of shades you would normally wear.

So, how do you go about choosing a new palette? You must study the original colours and establish two things: first, the relationships between the colours used, and second, the value of these colours.

The value of a colour is its comparison to a range of greys that run from white through to black. The best way to explain this is to think of a black and white photograph – a black and white photo turns the real life colours into relative values of grey, some lighter and some darker than others. A black and white film or a black and white photocopy would do the same thing.

1

2

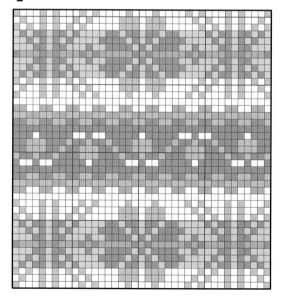

To establish the value of the colours used in the original palette, a simple solution is to make a little shade card of the colours used and run it through a photocopier. This will show you the colours in shades of grey, and you will then be able to start examining the relationship between the values. A successful Fair Isle will use colours that range in value from the lighter end of the scale through to the darker end.

Using a colour wheel

So, let's look at the colours used in our design **(3)**. There are five colours in total – a red, a cream, a pink, a blue and a beige. The top swatch **(4)** shows these five colours in their original state, and underneath you can see their value – their relative greys **(5)**. The red is the darkest and the cream is the lightest and the other colours lie in between. You could perhaps have guessed that the red and cream would be the darkest and lightest, but the beige and pink might surprise you – they are very close to each other in value, but to the naked eye you might be inclined to think that the pink was a lot darker than the beige when in fact there is very little in it. Charts **1** and **2** on the previous page show both the original colours and their comparative shades of grey. This helps to demonstrate the placement of the values within the design.

We've established the value, so now we need to establish the relationships between these five colours, and we are going to use the colour wheel to help us.

There are twelve sections on our colour wheel **(6)**, comprising of warm and cool colours. Warm colours advance towards the eye, and cool colours tend to recede. There are of course many more relationships – not just warm and cool – but this is enough to help us with our re-colouring exercise.

In our original palette we have two warm colours (red and pink), one cool colour (blue), and two neutrals (beige and cream). Neutrals don't feature on the colour wheel, but can be used in a number of ways, most often to help give balance. Here they have provided a vital balance in the values of the palette.

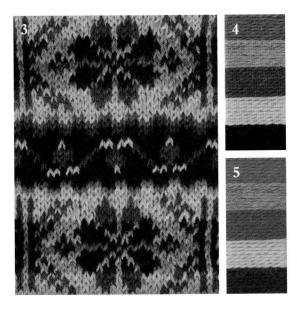

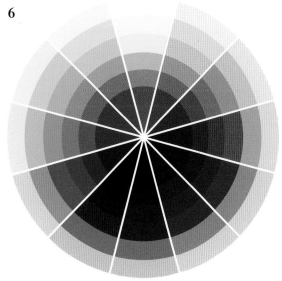

How value works

So, let's look at just what we have discovered so far. We have five colours that have a good range of values – a very dark through to a very light – and we know that two of the colours are warm, one is cool and two are neutral. Finding another five colours that mirror these qualities should give us a successful palette with which to substitute for the original colours.

In the swatch below (7) we have chosen a pink and a plum as our warm colours, a lime green as our cool and a chocolate brown and a light grey as our neutrals.

We have run the colours (8) through the copier to check their values (9) and they are a close match to the original. This then helps us to see which colour needs to be substituted for which, as we are going to substitute according to the relative values – the chocolate brown is going to be used instead of the red, the plum instead of the beige, the pink instead of the pink (that'll be easy to remember!), lime green instead of the blue and the light grey instead of the cream. The final result is a well balanced palette which is very different from the original, but which works due to the mirroring of the original relationships.

Warm and cool relationships

Warm palette

To highlight the importance of what we have discussed, let's look at a not-so-successful palette. We have chosen five colours, but this time we've paid attention to the value but not the colour relationships.

We have chosen three warm colours, one cool and one neutral (11). The values are close to the original palette (12), but the final result (10) is a little overpowering due to the increased number of warm colours.

As warm colours advance towards the eye, the palette is a little confusing – your eye is unsure where to look first. The fact that we have stayed true to the values of the original palette means it's not a complete disaster, but it could certainly be improved through a better balance of warm and cool.

Value clearly plays an important part in Fair Isle, so let's look at what can be achieved through value alone.

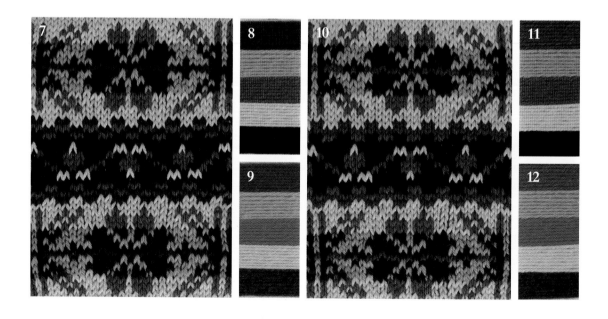

Cool palette

Here we have chosen five colours – navy blue, light blue, dark green, olive green and a very pale lime green, all of which are cool **(13)**. The fact that they are all cool removes the need for us to look at colour relationships and allows us to focus purely on the value. You can see that the values of these five colours are a close match to the original palette **(14+15)**.

If we then substitute each one according to their relative value, we have created another successful palette – this time through value alone.

Balanced neutrals

Another example of the importance of value in Fair Isle is when we want to create a palette from neutrals alone. In the final swatch below **(16)** we have chosen five different neutrals – a dark chocolate brown, a cream, a beige and two mid browns.

We have checked the values of these colours and there is a good range (like the original) which has resulted in a successful neutral palette **(17+18)**. If you were to ignore the values of colours, you would be in danger of using too many dark colours or too many light colours – which would result in an unbalanced palette.

Time to experiment

We have been specifically looking at how to re-colour an existing Fair Isle palette and have concluded that value is the key to its success (a good balance of light, dark and mid values) and that looking at colour relationships is also important. We've made our substitutions according to their relative values, but why not try moving the colours around within the design too?

There are many more colour relationships to explore (we've only just touched on warm and cool) and with all aspects of colour, the possibilities for experimenting are endless!

You might want to convey a certain mood with colour – to create a summery palette that evokes memories of sunny afternoons, warm colours will serve you well, or to create a feeling of calm, a cool palette will work. Think about what you want to achieve with your palette and then set about making choices based on the qualities of the original. Remember that colour is very personal and if you like it, go with it! Swatching is key to getting great results, so give it a go – there are hours of fun to be had.

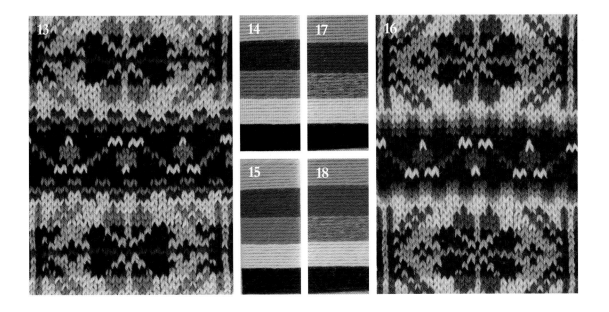

CHIC SPRING BERET
Jane Crowfoot

This sweet little hat in spring shades is knitted using two-handed Fair Isle. Converging columns of decreases accentuate the pretty stitch pattern. The variegated background colour lifts the pattern and adds interest.

This slouchy-styled Fair Isle beret, designed exclusively for *The Knitter* magazine by Jane Crowfoot, is a sweet accessory for cool spring days. It looks great worn with both short hair or long hair and flatters most faces – the young and not so young!

The beret is knitted using the technique of two-handed Fair Isle in the round, which we explore in detail on page 86.

'It's a great introduction to two-handed Fair Isle, because there are only three stitches between every colour change,' says Jane. 'This means that you won't have to do any weaving in – the yarn can simply be carried at the back of the work. It also means that you can keep track of your pattern repeat very easily.'

Jane advises that when holding the second colour in your left hand, be careful not to pull the yarn too tightly as this may cause puckering.

The pretty beret is knitted in four delicate shades of Patons Smoothie DK. It's a very soft yarn with a beautiful sheen, and is great value, too. We love Jane's blend of subtle tones in cream, khaki, lavender and lime, which is striking without being too bold.

SIZE
To fit average-sized adult's head

YARN
Patons Smoothie DK (100% acrylic; 100g/200m balls)
A Cream Mix (02100) 1 x 100g ball
B Khaki (01059) 1 x 100g ball
C Lime (01010) 1 x 100g ball
D Lavender (01050) 1 x 100g ball

NEEDLES
1 set of five 3.25mm (UK 10/US 3) double-pointed needles
1 set 4mm (UK 8/US 6) circular needles, no longer than 60cm
Stitch marker

TENSION
23 sts and 27 rows to 10cm over Fair Isle pattern using 4mm needles

Pattern

Using 3.25mm double-pointed needles and yarn A, cast on 108 sts. Distribute sts evenly across four of the five DPNs and join in the round, making sure that you have not twisted the sts around the needles, and place marker.

Rnd 1: ★K1, P1; rep from ★ to end of round.
Continue to work rib on the sts as set for a further 9 rounds.

Change to 4mm circular needles.

Next rnd: Change to yarn B. Knit 1 round.
Next rnd: (Increase) K4, ★M1, K4; rep from ★ to end of round. 134 sts.
Next rnd: (Increase) K4, ★M1, K6; rep from ★ to last 4 sts, M1, K4. 156 sts.
Next rnd: (Increase) K7, ★M1, K13; rep from ★ to last 6 sts, M1, K6. 168 sts. This completes the increases.

Work 4 more knit rounds in yarn B.

Beginning with chart row 1 and reading the chart from right to left, work the next 25 rounds using the Fair Isle technique.

You will work the pattern repeat a total of 7 times across the round, so you may find it easier to mark each pattern repeat of 24 sts.

Next rnd (chart rnd 26): (Decrease) Working from the chart, continue using the Fair Isle technique. When you reach the centre 3 sts of each pattern repeat, you need to decrease. To do this, slip a stitch knitwise, K2tog, pass slip stitch over (Sl 1, K1, psso) as shown on the chart. Continue to decrease in this way every alternate round where indicated on the chart.
 At round 32 change to 3.25mm DPNs and continue to work from chart.

(If you find that your stitches are stretching across the 4mm circular needles earlier than row 32, then you can switch to DPNs sooner otherwise you are in danger of stretching your knitting.)

Once you have completed round 47 you should be left with just 14 sts.
Next rnd: K2tog to end. 7 sts.

Making Up

Cut your yarn. Using a large sewing needle, thread the yarn end through the open sts and pull to tighten. Sew the yarn down inside the beret. Weave in all ends.

KEY

Patons Smoothie DK

⊡ 02100 (A) cream mix
☒ 01059 (B) khaki
☒ 01010 (C) lime
▼ 01050 (D) lavender
▨ no stitch
☐ sl1, k2tog, psso

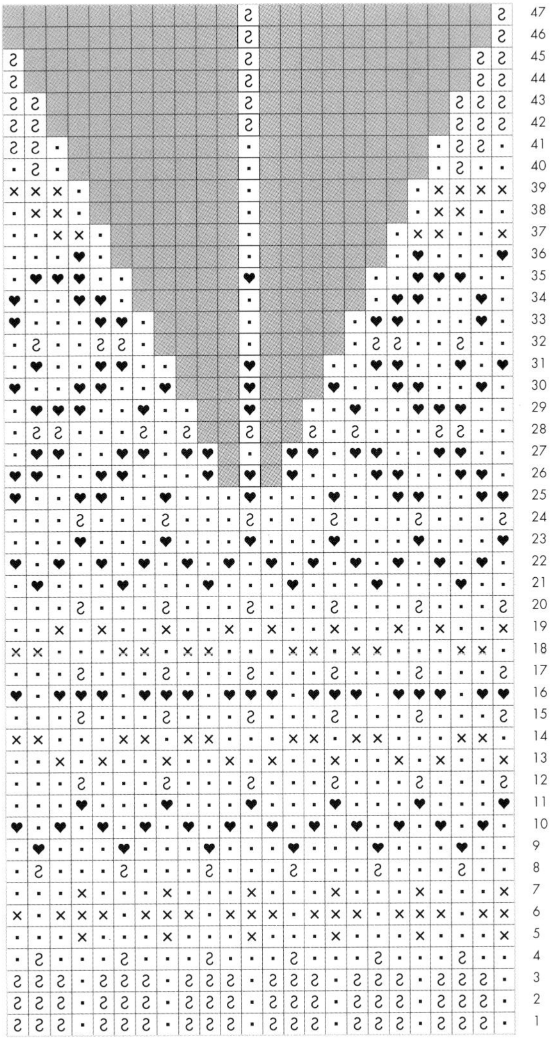

7 SHAPING & FIT

Here, we'll show you how to ensure you make the right decisions about your knitting projects. We'll explain how to measure your body, how to choose the correct size and how to make sure things fit.

THE PERFECT FIT
Jane Crowfoot

If you saw a lovely dress on a model in a magazine, would you buy it without trying it on? If you wanted an outfit for a wedding, would you choose it from the pages of a catalogue, then pop it in the wardrobe and assume it fitted you, without checking before the special occasion? Hopefully your answer to both these questions is 'Of course not!'

So why then, when choosing a pattern to knit, do so many of us assume that the knitted garment will fit us perfectly?

There's an amazing yarn shop in Paris called La Droguerie. It's only a small shop near to the Pompidou centre, but it is an absolute joy to behold. Inside there are glass jars of buttons and beads everywhere and the yarn hangs in hanks from hooks on the wall in all shades and textures. However, there is hardly a knitting pattern in sight.

While it's traditional for knitters in the UK to use patterns for most of their work, our counterparts in other countries often take a more relaxed approach, altering patterns or foregoing them entirely. Sales assistants overseas may even write up a quick pattern on the back of a yarn ball band and hand it over with your purchase.

While we're not suggesting that you abandon patterns, developing the confidence to make minor changes can result in a better fit and a more successful outcome.

How to measure your body

To do this properly you'll need the help of a friend. Wear a relatively tight-fitting vest or T-shirt, and some shorts or leggings (if you're feeling brave, strip to your knickers). Use a tape measure that shows both inch and centimetre measurements.

Using a sharp pencil and plain paper, draw a sketch of your body on which you can mark all your measurements. There are some great examples online that can be downloaded for free (for example, from www.fashion-era.com/elegant_fashion_templates.htm).

Take some time to identify the places on your body that your friend will measure. To be really accurate, mark these (gently) with a washable marker pen. When being measured, remember to stand up straight.

1 **Back neck:** Feeling with your fingers down the vertebrae at the top of your spine, you should feel a bone that is more prominent than the others towards the base of your neck. You may find that this is where the neckline of a close-fitting T-shirt would normally sit, or where your necklaces lie.

Waist: This is the thinnest part of your body between the bottom of your ribcage and your hip bones – it's not necessarily in line with your navel.

Hips: Most women assume their hips to be the widest part of their bodies; however, with many of us, the widest part is our bottom. To locate your hips, feel for the iliac crests, which are the parts of your pelvis that stick out at the front. Mark the base of your back in line with these bones.

Bottom: This is measured at its widest place. Mark your body in line with this point.

Bust: This is the widest point of your bust. Be aware that your underwear can influence this measurement.

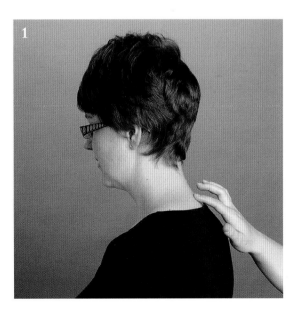

1

2   **Mid back:** Stand with your arms out straight and make a mark at the centre point of your back between your shoulder blades and in line with your raised arms. **Wrist:** Identify the prominent bone on your wrist where your hand joins your arm. Use this bone to mark the position of your wrist.

Take the following measurements and add them to your body sketch:

3   **Mid back to wrist**

4   **Back neck to waist**
    Back neck to hips
    Back neck to bottom
    Bust

5   **Waist**

6   **Hips**
    Bottom

Sizing explained

Clothes are usually made to standard sizes. In the UK, clothes typically use one of two sizing methods. The numbered system for women runs from a size 4 through to 24 and above. We also have worded sizes such as small, medium and large. The latter has traditionally been used in relation to knitting patterns, which is unfortunate as this is

a very unclear way of sizing as the dimensions of the pieces are determined by the designer and can vary from one to another. Thankfully, many of the well-known yarn brands and designers have made a concerted effort to design to the numbered system.

Choosing the correct size

There are thousands of women in this country who would choose a size 12 – and yet all will have different body shapes. They could be nearer the lofty heights of six foot tall, or have an ample bosom and hourglass shape. In theory, if we were all to try on the same garment in the same size, it wouldn't fit the same on any two of us.

So, let us now apply this theory to the practice of choosing which size knitting pattern to follow.

On the right you will find the sizing guide for a knitted top (Sublime's Thai Top). You will see that you are given three measurements to go by (notice that 'Actual Bust' is smaller than the 'To Fit Bust' measurement due to the tight-fitting nature of the garment).

Once you have identified the size that you think is closest to your body size, check the following three things to ensure that you have chosen correctly:

Check your sketch: When deciding which size to choose, first compare the size measurements to your body sketch, noting how wide and how long your chosen size will come out.

Check your wardrobe: It's useful to measure the dimensions of a garment from your wardrobe, such as a

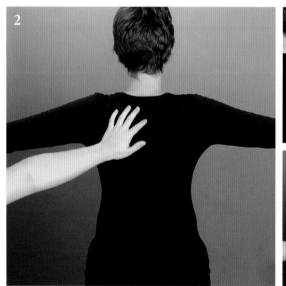

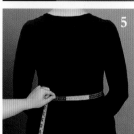

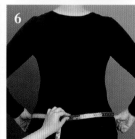

T-shirt **(1, above)**. (Your chosen garment doesn't need to be knitted, but a slightly stretchy fabric such as jersey is ideal.) You may be surprised by how big your garments actually are, but don't be alarmed – it is better to have a slightly bigger garment with a nice fit than something that comes up too small.

   Check your body: Ask a friend to measure the length of the garment in comparison to your body to show you where the garment will finish.

   With these three steps taken into account, you can now go ahead and choose the size that comes closest to your own dimensions.

	8	10	12	14	16	18	
To Fit	81	86	91	97	102	107	cm
Bust	32	34	36	38	40	42	in
Actual	77	83	88	94	99	105	cm
Bust	30¼	32¾	34¾	37	39	41½	in
Finished	56	58	59	60	62	64	cm
Length	22	22¾	23¼	23¾	24¼	25¼	in

Sleeve length

Many knitting patterns are accompanied by a blocking diagram – a line drawing showing the full dimensions of the knitted garment, including sleeve length. However, some patterns may not give you this information.

   To find out the sleeve length and thus decide whether you need to make any changes to the pattern, read through the pattern and establish the following:

   How long the sleeve is AFTER all shaping is completed and BEFORE armhole decreasing is started.

   Take the actual bust measurement and divide this figure by 4.

   Add this number to the sleeve length.

Compare this answer to your mid back to wrist measurement and add approx 2.5cm. This will be your ideal sleeve length to your wrist.

Note: The bust measurement on a blocking diagram is usually the measurement for each of the two pieces that make up the garment, and not an actual bust measurement – in this case you must divide the number by 2, and not 4.

Changing a pattern to the shape of your body

Very few of us are a standard size 12 or 14 (for example). In fact, many of us fall between two sizes and it's therefore common for knitters to be disappointed with the fit of a finished garment. To illustrate how a few minor changes to a knitting pattern make a big difference in terms of fit, we will show you two garments on the same model.

Garment One in red

Based on her measurements, our model, Jen, felt she would normally have chosen to knit the size 14. No changes were made to this pattern.

   The top fits well at the shoulders and middle, but it pulls a little across the bust and hips **(1, below)**. Jen chose the size 14 because she thought her bust measurement was closest to the 'to fit' size 14 measurement. This garment has been designed with negative ease, so the actual bust measurement is smaller that the 'to fit' measurement.

   Jen's bust is a little larger than the size 14, which, in combination with the negative ease, means that the size 14 top doesn't fit very well in this area **(2)**.

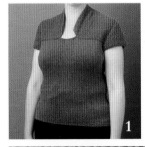
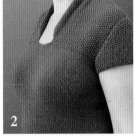

The same number of stitches are cast on at the hem as are present at the bust section. This means that the hip actual measurement for the size 14 will also be 94cm. This is noticeably less than Jen's actual hip measurement, hence the poor fit in this area **(3)**.

Garment Two in green

For this garment, we discussed with Jen what changes she felt were needed – which we made in little more than an hour.

Measurements and decisions

We measured Jen's bust, waist and hips. Our first suggestion to Jen was that we make our changes to the size 16 and not the 14. This was a decision based on her bust size (98cm), as well as the actual bust measurement of the garment. By knitting a bust size too small, the garment will also shrink in length because the fabric is being used to stretch horizontally and can't simultaneously stretch in length.

We can calculate the waist measurement for the size 16 from the stitch count and tension information. The stitch count for size 16 was 188 after waist shaping is completed. The stitch tension is 22 sts to 10cm. 22 divided by 10 gives 2.2 sts per cm. You can then divide the stitch count by 2.2 to tell you how many cm the waist will measure: 188 divided by 2.2 gives us 85.5cm. Jen's waist measurement was a little more than this, so we decided to remove some of the waist decreases.

Jen's hip measurement is 107cm, so basing the pattern on the size 16 will improve the fit at the hips **(4)**. The actual hip measurement for the size 16 is 99cm, the same as the bust measurement.

When Jen measured down her back, she decided that she wanted the garment to sit in line with her hips. The size 16 has a length of 62cm, but Jen was happier with a slightly shorter length. We decided to opt for a length of 58/59cm to make sure that Jen's top was not likely to 'part company' with the top of her waistband. This also ensures that the garment won't ride up. We decided to leave neckline shaping and sleeves as for the pattern.

How we calculated the changes

The first thing we did was work out a stitch and row count to 1cm. To do this, we divided the tension by 10cm. (22 sts and 28 rows to 10cm divided by 10 = 2.2 sts and 2.8 rows to 1cm.) These stitch and row counts must not be rounded up to whole numbers.

We calculated by how many stitches and rows we needed to change the pattern by multiplying the stitch and row count to 1cm by Jen's chosen measurements.

We kept the cast-on stitch count for the size 16 as it was in the pattern, but because Jen wanted the garment to be shorter, with better fit at the waist, we removed two of the shaping repeats, making the stitch count 196 instead of 188 at the waist.

We left the number of straight rows at the waist the same as the pattern, but by removing two lots of shaping between the hip and waist, we made Jen's piece 14 rows shorter than the pattern. This represents 5cm, which is just about the difference in length that Jen wanted to achieve.

It was essential that Jen increased the bust to the correct number of stitches **(5)**. The original pattern has six increase repeats, but we changed the stitch count at the

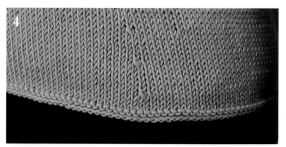

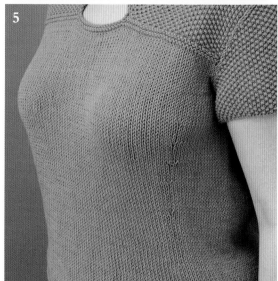

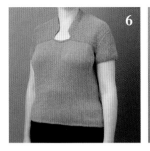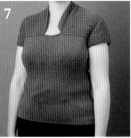

waist, which meant we had to recalculate the bust shaping. Therefore, instead of increasing seven times on every seventh row (as in the original pattern) we increased five times on every 11th row.

From the underarm onwards, Jen followed the original pattern.

The second garment (6), adjusted from the size 16 pattern, fits much better than the standard size 14 (7) at the hips and bust. Jen was very pleased with the improved fit of the top. Hopefully this will inspire you to make tweaks to patterns and improve the fit of your own projects.

Note: It was essential that Jen achieved the correct tension. We also advised her to try the piece on as much as possible as she knitted, to check that the changes were working.

How to change a pattern by one size (sizing up or down)

To illustrate how to size up or size down a pattern, we are once again going to use the example of the Thai top.

Step One: Looking at the standard sizes, we can see that the bust measurement of a size 10 is 6cm larger than that of a size 8. A size 12 is another 6cm bigger. Between sizes 14 and 16 the difference is 5cm, and it's the same between a 16 and an 18. We can therefore assume that if we wanted to knit a size smaller than 8 we would take 6cm away from the bust measurement and if we want a size larger than 18 then we would add another 5cm.

Actual Bust	77	83	88	94	99	105	cm
	30¼	32¾	34¾	37	39	41½	in
Finished Length	56	58	59	60	62	64	cm
	22	22¾	23¼	23¾	24¼	25¼	in

Step Two: (How many stitches to cast on) 'Using 3.25mm circular needles, cast on 168 (180:192:204:216:228) sts.'

Looking at the number of stitches cast on for the body, above, we can see that there are 12 sts more cast on for every size from 8 up. So then, if we want to knit a size smaller than the size 8 we will cast on 12 sts fewer. If we want to knit a size bigger than 18 then we will cast on 12 sts more than the stitch count for that size.

As long as we don't wish to alter the shaping of the garment, we can simply go through the pattern with a pencil and write in our new stitch counts. We may have to do a bit of maths to work out the neckline shaping, but it shouldn't differ too much from the next size up or down. If you're happy to keep the neckline the same as the nearest size, you can simply include half of the extra (or fewer) stitches on each side of the shoulders.

Step Three: (Changing the length) If we look at the standard sizes once more, we can see that the overall length differs between sizes by 1–2cm. If we decide to knit a size smaller than the size 8 then we will need to knit our piece 1cm shorter. If we decide to knit a size bigger than the 18, we will need to add 2cm to the length. The best place to do this is after the cast on and/or just before armhole shaping.

Step Four: (Armhole shaping) Looking at armhole shaping, we can see that there's also a logical grading of the pattern at this point. The stitch count here changes by 6 stitches between every size and the measurement from start of armhole shaping changes by 1cm between most sizes. A 19cm drop is average for a size 8 and a 23cm drop is average for a size 18. We would suggest that a size smaller than 8 retains the 19cm drop and that a size bigger than 18 sticks to a 23cm drop. Thus the sleeve for the next size up or down will fit the body of your amended garment.

Step Five: (Yarn amounts) If you change the size of your piece, you will use a different amount of yarn from that quoted in the pattern. In the case of the Thai top, this only varies a little. A size 8 uses six balls and a size smaller would be likely to use between five and six. The size 18 uses nine balls. To make the size bigger, we'll be adding quite a lot of fabric and although we'll probably only use one more ball, we suggest buying two extra just in case.

WAIST SHAPING
Belinda Boaden

Waist shaping is what many knitters look for in a garment – the subtle tailoring that gives a more flattering fit to the female figure. However, many knitting patterns for jumpers and cardigans do not have any waist shaping, so here we will explain the different ways to add shaping that is appropriate for your own body shape.

Modern shapes

So, if waist shaping is desirable to so many people, why don't more designs have it? Trends have a lot to answer for, but bear in mind that writing significant waist shaping into a pattern for general sizes from 8 to 22 – and making it fit and be flattering on all eight sizes – is nigh-on impossible because of the myriad different body shapes people have. Waist shaping in the wrong place for a body is even more unflattering than no waist shaping at all.

Your body measurements

1   The bust and hip measurements for most bodies are fairly constant; indeed, they are the basis for all clothes patterns, as with a little ease everyone can find something to fit. Body/torso length, on the other hand, varies wildly – there are long bodies, short bodies, some are thicker waisted, and it is these variables that make writing shaping into a generic, all-sizes pattern too problematic. The good news is that shaping is easy to add in if you know your own body shape. You must, however, have an accurate and honest idea of your own measurements.

2   So, possibly with the aid of a friend, and definitely using a good tape measure, you need the following measurements. Depending on the garment you want to modify, some measurements may be taken at different points of the body:
(a) Actual waist. This is always the measurement around the narrowest point between bust and hips. Keep the tape fairly taut, but allow a couple of centimetres of ease.
(b) Hip. This is one that may differ from garment to garment. A 'proper' hip measurement (for skirt/trouser purposes) is taken around the widest part of you, often more around the top of your thighs/bottom than around the 'hip bone'. For these purposes it needs to be the widest part of you that the garment will actually be covering, which is often much higher on the body as lots of knits aren't this long.

If your knit is quite long towards the tops of your legs, you might want to take two hip measurements: a 'high hip'(b) and a 'low hip' (f), and supplement these with a further vertical measurement between them (g). Keep the tape horizontal, and fairly taut but with a bit of ease.
(c) The vertical measurement between (a) and (b). This is where a friend and/or string tied around you can help a lot.
(d) Bust. Again, make sure the tape is properly horizontal when you measure.
(e) The vertical measurement between (a) and (d). Again, a friend or string and a mirror are useful.

If you then draw these measurements out on graph paper to scale, the following methods become much easier. Use one square per cm and divide (a), (b) and (d) by 2 to get a 'flat' measurement.

3   Our sample measurements here are made up for a bust and waist size between sizes 10/12, and hips between sizes 12/14, as many people are different 'standard' sizes at these points. Any pattern with generic shaping will probably have (c) and (e) as being equidistant, but you might find that they differ on your own measurements.

As you can see in our diagram, there is approximately 3cm straight at (c) – very few people go straight 'in and out', but if you do then draw it that way.

Changing needle size

The easiest way to add in slight waist shaping is to use needles of slightly differing sizes to alter the tension of the fabric. This will gently pull it in and then let it out again; we used this in the Carmine V-neck Jumper

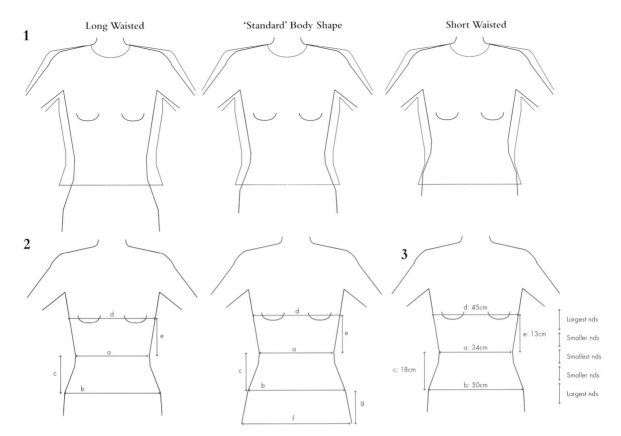

1   Long Waisted   'Standard' Body Shape   Short Waisted

2

3

d: 45cm — Largest nds

e: 13cm — Smaller nds

a: 34cm — Smallest nds

c: 18cm — Smaller nds

b: 50cm — Largest nds

design (page 106). So if the body of your pattern is knitted on 4.5mm needles, you would drop to 4mm, then 3.75mm and perhaps even 3.25mm needles (if you are very shapely around the waist) before going back through 3.75mm, 4mm and ending finally on 4.5mm needles again.

Where you need to change needle sizes is governed by your own measurements, although for this method it is not quite so important. For the measurements in 3 where (b) is the bottom hem of the garment, and if you wanted to use three different sizes of needles altogether, you would knit as per the pattern until the body measured 7cm, change needles, work a further 7cm, change needles, work approximately 5cm on these smallest needles, change back to your middle size, work another 5cm and then go back to the original size needles and carry on for the underarm shaping.

To demonstrate this we knitted a swatch 36 stitches wide; needle sizes are: 3.75mm (8 rows st st), 3.5mm (6 rows st st), 3.25mm (10 rows st st), then back to 3.5mm (6 rows again) and 3.75mm (another 7 rows and then cast off) **(4)**. As you can see, the change in tension between needle sizes is barely noticeable, but there is a gentle change in width from 16cm down to 15cm and then back to 16cm – obviously over the width of a whole garment, this would make a more noticeable waist shaping.

The absolute best bit about this method is that it will work over any pattern, cables, texture, colourwork and lace, whereas the next method we'll discuss might disrupt any patterning you have going on, or at the very least be noticeable.

Altering stitch counts

For the next method – altering the number of stitches in your garment – you will need an accurately measured tension swatch to go with your body measurements, a flat 'spec' drawing of the garment as the pattern is written and, possibly, a calculator.

We knitted a swatch again, this time with the entire swatch knitted on 3.75mm needles (1). Tension is 21.5 sts and 28 rows to 10cm. We will assume here that your pattern works the main body of the garment in stocking stitch and already allows for slightly bigger hip size than bust (so is very slightly A-line, as in 2; for these purposes we are not including any ribbing in the following calculations). This is how you would work out stitches to decrease: (required waist width in cm ÷ 10 [cm, the measurement over which tension was taken]) x stitch tension = number stitches required.

Using the measurements in 2, and adding a few centimetres ease at the waist to give us a 37cm width measurement, this gives:

(37 ÷ 10) x 21.5 = 79.55 stitches

So, depending on whether the pattern required you to cast on an even or odd number of stitches, we would round this down to 79 or up to 80 sts. As the pattern asks for a cast on of 112 sts, we'll round up to 80. Now we can work out how many stitches we want to decrease:

112 − 80 = 32 stitches

Divide this number by 2 to work out how many decrease rows we need:

32 ÷ 2 = 16 rows

Now we need to know how many rows to work these decreases over, so the formula would be:

(required length in cm ÷ 10) x row tension = number of rows to work, so (18 ÷ 10) x 28 = 50.4 rows which we would round down to 50 rows.

To work out when to decrease, we divide the number of rows you have by the number of decreases needed:

50 ÷ 16 = 3.125

Now, as 16 multiplied by 3 gives you 48, this fits quite nicely, although we wouldn't really want to decrease on every 3rd row as this would mean working decreases on wrong-side rows, so we'll say to decrease:

On the next row (RS) then (on the 4th, then following 2nd row) 7 times, then on the following 4th row once more.

So we have 2 decrease rows worked in 6 rows of knitting and we're decreasing on right-side rows only with a nice steady progression of decreases over 48 rows. You can draw these out on graph paper to help you visualise the workings if it helps (3).

Now to work out the increases. We need to increase back to 104 stitches over approx. 17cm. So, rows to increase in are:

(17 ÷ 10) x 28 = 47.6 rows which we will round up to 48 rows.

We have 80 stitches, we need 104, therefore we need to increase:

104 ÷ 80 = 24 stitches, divide by 2 for the number of increase rows and this gives us: 24 ÷ 2 = 12

12 increase rows within 48 total rows.

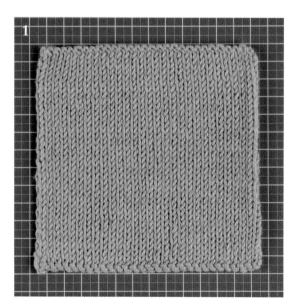

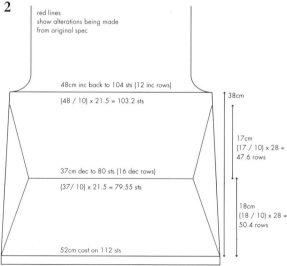

2

red lines
show alterations being made
from original spec

48cm inc back to 104 sts (12 inc rows)

(48 / 10) x 21.5 = 103.2 sts

38cm

17cm
(17 / 10) x 28 =
47.6 rows

37cm dec to 80 sts (16 dec rows)

(37/ 10) x 21.5 = 79.55 sts

18cm
(18 / 10) x 28 =
50.4 rows

52cm cast on 112 sts

Divide the number of rows by the number of increases:
48 ÷ 12 = 4

So we will increase every 4th row. Again, draw these out if it helps (upper part of **3**).

It is best to leave a few centimetres of straight knitting before you start the armhole decreases. If you look at your body, the widest bit of your bust is generally below where you would be starting to work armhole decreases. Again, this is a measurement that's very hard to approximate, especially if you take a larger cup size, but one that's fairly easy to allow for personally with a bit of thought.

So, onto the actual knitting of the decreases. The easiest way is to work them 2 or 3 stitches in from the edge of the garment, working a left-leaning decrease (SSK) and right-leaning decrease (K2tog) as paired decreases on each row (**4**).

However, if you want to make a feature of the shaping, work them further into the body of the garment – if you have quite a few decrease rows to work, as in the above example, and work them 6 or 8 stitches into the body, you should end up with a good-looking shaping 'line' which will also work to define your own curves and be flattering to wear (**5**).

Increases, too, work better if they are paired to appear on the inside of the 'edge' stitches – for example, working, M1R after the first 7 (in this case) stitches of the row and then M1L before the last 7 stitches (upper part of **5**). Working the increases an extra stitch in keeps the 'line' consistent.

Hopefully this will have explained some of the difficulties of writing generic waist shaping into patterns, but also given solutions as to how to add in your own shaping for a perfect fit. Lots of knitting is maths and measuring, but it's not really difficult once you sit down and try it - and it's well worth having a go!

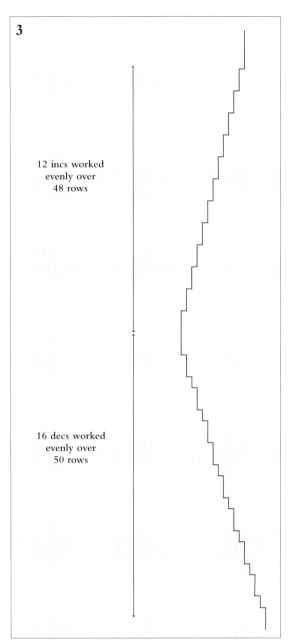

3

12 incs worked
evenly over
48 rows

16 decs worked
evenly over
50 rows

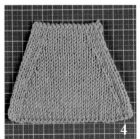

CARMINE V-NECK JUMPER
Belinda Boaden

This richly textured jumper in a soft, lustrous yarn is knitted from the top down.

Belinda Boaden's Carmine jumper has an opulent feel, thanks to the richly textured fabric and the lustrous Fyberspates Scrumptious DK merino/silk yarn in a delicious shade of cherry red.

The jumper has a feminine, fitted shape with a deep V-neck and three-quarter-length sleeves. The stretchy nature of the fabric means it will hug your figure; try pairing it with a silk skirt or pair of smart trousers for a glamorous yet comfortable effect.

It is knitted from the top down, starting with the shoulders. Increases are worked on the back, front, sleeves and at the V-neck, before the work is then split for the body and sleeves. As the increases are worked in different places on different rounds, Belinda has prepared a helpful increase table so that you can tick off each row as it is completed.

The stitch pattern is worked over 14 stitches and uses a combination of false cable motifs. When you are increasing, you will need to use stocking stitch until you have enough stitches to work the whole motif, with reverse stocking stitch between motifs.

SIZE

	8	10	12	14	16	18	20	22	
To Fit	81	86	91	97	102	107	112	117	cm
Bust	32	34	36	38	40	42	44	46	in
Actual	76	80	86	91	97	102	107	112	cm
Bust	30	31½	33	35	38	40	42	44	in
Actual	52½	54	56	59	60½	63	64½	65½	cm
Length	20½	21½	22	23	23½	25	25½	25½	in
Sleeve	29	30	30	31	31	31	32	32	cm
Seam	11½	12	12	12¼	12¼	12¼	12½	½	in

YARN
Fyberspates Scrumptious DK (55% merino wool, 45% silk; 220m/100g skeins)

| **Cherry** | 4 | 4 | 5 | 5 | 5 | 5 | 6 | 6 | x 100g skeins |

NEEDLES & ACCESSORIES
1 set 3.75mm (UK 9/US 5) circular needles, 80cm long
1 set 4.5mm (UK 7/US 7) circular needles, 80cm long
1 set 3.75mm (UK 9/US 5) double-pointed needles
1 set 4.5mm (UK 7/US 7) double-pointed needles, or smaller circular needles in the same sizes if you wish to knit the sleeves in the round, otherwise 1 pair of each size of straight needles
Stitch holders
Stitch markers

TENSION
25 sts and 31 rows to 10cm over pattern using 4.5mm needles, with pattern completely relaxed

SPECIAL ABBREVIATIONS
twyo: Twisted yarn over: place a backward loop on the needle (as if to cast on 1 st)

PATTERN NOTES
Increase table on page 108 shows which rows have increases worked on back, fronts, sleeves and V-neck edges. Mark off rows as you work them, to keep track of the increases. All increases are taken into the 14-st pattern repeat, which is shown separately in Chart B. If you don't have enough sts to work a whole stitch motif, replace the partial motif with stocking st.

Shoulders

Using 3.75mm needles cast on 89 (89:89:97:97:105:105:
111) sts.
Work WS set-up row from chart for your size (charts Ai–
Aiv), placing markers as foll:
4 sts (Right Front), pm, 1 st (seam st), pm, 21
(21:21:21:23:23:25:25:27) sts (Right Sleeve), pm, 1 st (seam
st), pm, 35 (35:35:39:39:43:43:45) sts (Back), pm, 1 st (seam
st), pm, 21 (21:21:23:23:25:25:27) sts (Left Sleeve), pm, 1 st
(seam st), 4 sts (Left Front).

All increases are worked with a backward loop
increase, where you place a backward loop of yarn on the
needle (like a twisted yarn over). This stitch is not then
worked until the following row. Increases on sleeves, back
and fronts are worked adjacent to the marked seam stitch.
The V-neck increases are worked at the start and end of
the row.

All increases are taken into the 14-st pattern (shown
separately in chart B), with the exception of the 2 final
V-neck increases for sizes 14–22, which need to be worked
as the single stitch wavy cable, followed by a purl stitch.

Increase table shows on which rows to work back (B),
front (F), sleeve (S) and V-neck (V) increases.

Now working from increase table and chart for your
size (charts Ai–Aiv), work first 4 rows of pattern on smaller
needles, then change to 4.5mm needles and continue until
44 (48:52:54:56:58:60:62) rows of pattern have been
worked.

Between the seam sts, you should have the following
for each section:
Back: 77 (81:87:93:99:105:109:115) sts.
Sleeves: 51 (53:55:57:61:63:65:67) sts.
Fronts: 36 (38:41:44:48:49:52:55) sts.
Total: 255 (267:283:299:321:333:347:363) sts (including
4 seam sts).

Split body from sleeves

Continuing to work increases at V-neck as per table, split
sleeves from body as foll:
Row 45 (49:53:55:57:59:61:63): Working V inc on sizes
18 and 22, patt 88 (92:97:102:110:114:118:124) sts taking
you to the end of the first sleeve, turn.

Left sleeve

*Cast on 7 (7: 7:8:8:8:9:9) sts, patt 51 (53:55:57:61:63:
65:67) sts, turn, cast on 7 (7:7:8:8:8:9:9) sts.
65 (67:69:73:77:79:83:85) sts.

Take cast on sts into patt as set, working rev st st until there
are enough sts to work patt. Work on these sts only for left
sleeve (put rem sts on a holder), dec as foll:
Dec 1 st at each end of 7th and 2 (3:6:8:2:12:11:10) foll
10th (10th:8th:8th:8th:8th:6th:6th:6th) rows.
59 (59:55:55:71:53:59:63) sts.
Then dec 1 st at each end of 7 (6:4:3:11:4:4:6) foll 8th
(8th:6th:6th:6th:4th:4th:4th) rows. 45
(47:47:49:49:49:51:51) sts.

Change to smaller needles and cont without shaping until
sleeve meas 29 (30:30:31:31:31:32:32) cm.
Cast off evenly and not too tightly in patt.

Right sleeve

With RS facing, rejoin yarn to back sts. Patt across 130
(136:144:152:162:170:176:184) sts, taking you to end of
right sleeve, turn. Work Right Sleeve as for Left from *.

Body

With RS facing, rejoin yarn to rem front sts, and
(remembering V-neck inc in sizes 18 and 22), patt 37
(39:42:45:49:51:53:57) sts to end of row. Turn.

Row 46 (50:54:56:58:60:62:64) (WS): Patt 37 (39:42:45:49:51:53:57) sts, cast on 14 (14:14:16:16:16:18:18) sts , patt 79 (83:89:95:101:107:109:115) sts (seam st, back sts and seam st), cast on 14 (14:14:16:16:16:18:18) sts, patt 37 (39:42:45:49:51:53:57). 181 (189:201:217:231:241:251:265) sts.

Work fronts and back as set previously, and follow chart for appropriate size (charts Bi–Bviii) for how to work underarm cast on sts (and seam sts where appropriate). Charts show direction to work rows at each underarm. Cont to work V-neck shaping as shown in increase table, until you have worked the row marked END.

Row 57 (61:65:67:69:71:73:75): Join to work in the round as foll. Place stitches onto a circular needle (if not already), placing last st of round between the 1st and 2nd sts of round (the 2 purl sts at centre front). Purl these 2 sts tog, pattern around making sure to work patt as given on the chart for working in the round now.

Work straight until body section measures 9½ (10:11:12:13:14:14½:14½) cm from split from sleeves.

Change to 3.75mm needles and work a further 11½ (12:12:12:12:12:12:12½) cm.
Change back to 4.5mm needle and work a further 12cm.
Change to 3.75mm needle again and work another 3cm.
Cast off loosely and evenly in pattern.

Neckband

With RS facing and using 3.75mm circular needles, starting at left back shoulder seam st, pick up and knit 21 (21:21:23:23:25:25:27) sts across left sleeve top, 41 (42:42:44:44:45:45:46) sts down left front neck, 1 st from central point of 'V' (mark this stitch), 41 (42:42:44:44:45:45:46) sts up right front neck, 21 (21:21:23:23:25:25:27) sts across right sleeve top and 35 (35:35:39:39:43:43:46) sts across back neck. 160 (162:162:174:174:184:184: 193) sts.

Purl 1 round.
Next rnd: Purl to 2 sts before marked stitch, P2tog, purl marked stitch, P2tog tbl, purl to end of round. 158 (160:160:172:172:182:182:191) sts.
Next rnd: Purl. Repeat these 2 rounds once more. 156 (158:158:170:170:180:180:189) sts.
Cast off neatly purlwise.

Sew sleeve seams and underarm seam. Block gently to measurements, following any yarn care instructions on the ball band.

Row	8	10	12	14	16	18	20	22	row
1	BFS	BFS	BFS	BFS	BF	BF	BF	BFS	1
2					VS		S		2
3	V	BF	BF	BF	BF	BFVS	BF	BFV	3
4	BFS	S	VS	VS			V		4
5		BF	BF	BF	BFS	BF	BFS	bfs	5
6					V	S			6
7	BFVS	BFVS	BF	BF	BF	BF	bf	bf	7
8			S	VS	S	V	vs	Vs	8
9	BF	BF	BFV	BF	BFV	BFS	bf	bf	9
10	S	S							10
11	BFV	BFV	BFS	BFS	BFS	BF	bfs	bfs	11
12				V		S	v		12
13	BFS	BFS	BFV	BF	BFV	BFVS	bf	bfV	13
14			S	S	VS		s	s	14
15	BFV	BFV	BF	BF	BF	BFS	bf	bf	15
16	S	S		V			v		16
17	BF	BF	BFS	BFS	BFS	BF	bfs	bfs	17
18			V		V	VS		V	18
19	BFVS	BFVS	BF	BF	BF	BF	bf	bf	19
20			S	VS	S		vs	s	20
21	BF	BF	BF	bf	BF	BFS	bf	bf	21
22	S	S		V	V				22
23	BFV	BFV	BFS	BFS	BFS	BFV	bfs	bfvs	23
24				V		S	v		24
25	BFs	BFS	BF	BF	BF	BF	bf	bf	25
26			S	S	VS				26
27	BFV	BFV	BFV	BF	BF	BFVS	bf	bfv	27
28	S	S		V			v		28
29	BF	BF	BFS	BFS	BFS	BF	bfs	bfs	29
30					V	s			30
31	BFVS	BFVS	BFV	BF	BF	BFV	bf	bfv	31
32			S	VS	S		vs	s	32
33	BF	BF	BF	BF	BF	BFS	bf	bf	33
34			S		V				34
35	BFVS	BFV	BFS	BFS	BFS	BFV	bfs	bfvs	35
36			V	V		S	v		36
37	BF	BFS	BF	BF	BF	BF	bf	bf	37
38	S		S	S	VS		sv		38
39	BFV	BFV	BF	BF	BF	BFVS	bf	bf	39
40		S	V	V			v		40
41	BFS	BF	BFS	BFS	BFS	BF	bfs	bfs	41
42					V	S		v	42
43	BFVS	BFVS	BF	BF	BF	bfv	bf	bf	43
44			S	VS	s		vs	s	44
45	*	BF	BFV	BF	bf	bfs	bf	bfv	45
46		S			v				46
47	V	V	BFS	BFS	bfs	bfv	bfs	bfs	47
48				V		s	v	bf	48
49		*	BFV	BF	bf	bf	bf	bfv	49
50					bfvs		bfs	s	50
51	V	V	BFS	BFS	bf	bfvs	bf	bf	51
52			V		s	bf	v	bfv	52
53			*	BF	bf	bf	bfs	bfs	53
54	V		V		bfv	s	bf		54
55		V		*	bfs	bfv	bf	bf	55
56	END			V		bf	vs	bfvs	56
57				*	bfs	bf	bf		57
58			V		v		bf		58
59		V		V		v*	bfvs	bfvs	59
60		END					bf		60
61						*	bf		61
62			V	V					62
63			V		V		v*		63
64			END			v			64
65				V					65
66			END	V		v			66
67				V					67
68				END					68
69					v				69
70				END	v				70
71					bf				71
72					END				72
73					v				73
74					END				74

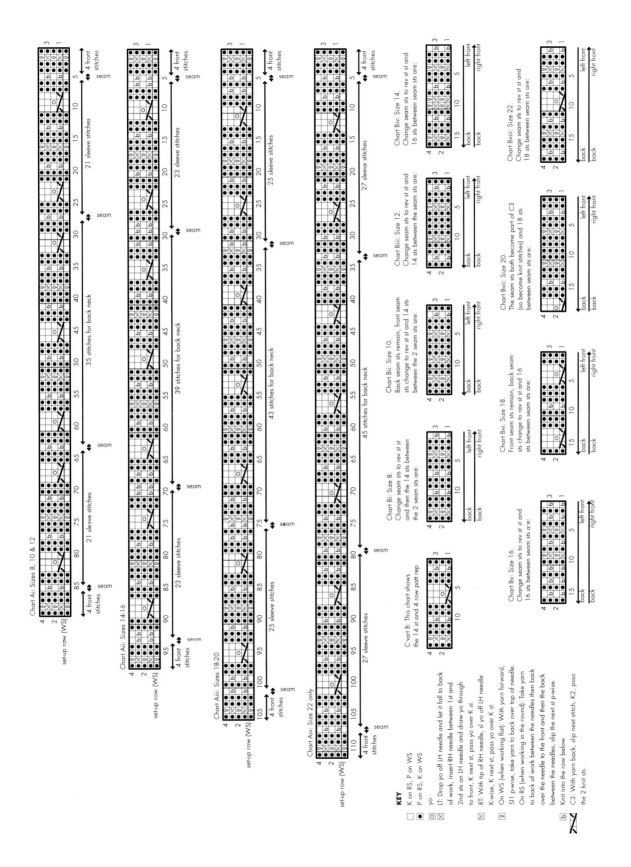

Chart Ai: Sizes 8, 10 & 12

set-up row (WS)

21 sleeve stitches

35 stitches for back neck

21 sleeve stitches

4 front stitches

seam

4 front stitches

Chart Aii: Sizes 14-16

set-up row (WS)

23 sleeve stitches

39 stitches for back neck

23 sleeve stitches

4 front stitches

seam

4 front stitches

Chart Aiii: Sizes 18-20

set-up row (WS)

25 sleeve stitches

43 stitches for back neck

25 sleeve stitches

4 front stitches

seam

4 front stitches

Chart Aiv: Size 22 only

set-up row (WS)

27 sleeve stitches

45 stitches for back neck

27 sleeve stitches

4 front stitches

seam

4 front stitches

Chart B: This chart shows the 14 st and 4 row patt rep

Chart Bi: Size 8.
Change seam sts to rev st st and then the 14 sts between the 2 seam sts are:

left front
right front
back
back

Chart Bii: Size 10.
Back seam sts remain, front seam sts change to rev st st and 14 sts between the 2 seam sts are:

left front
right front
back
back

Chart Biii: Size 12.
Change seam sts to rev st st and 14 sts between the seam sts are:

left front
right front
back
back

Chart Biv: Size 14.
Change seam sts to rev st st and 16 sts between the seam sts are:

left front
right front
back
back

Chart Bv: Size 16.
Change seam sts to rev st st and 16 sts between seam sts are:

left front
right front
back
back

Chart Bvi: Size 18.
Front seam sts remain, back seam sts change to rev st st and 16 sts between seam sts are:

left front
right front
back
back

Chart Bvii: Size 20.
The seam sts both become part of C3 (so become knit stitches) and 18 sts between seam sts are:

left front
right front
back
back

Chart Bviii: Size 22.
Change seam sts to rev st st and 18 sts between seam sts are:

left front
right front
back
back

KEY

☐ K on RS, P on WS

● P on RS, K on WS

○ ⊠ yo

⊠ LT: Drop yo off LH needle and let it fall to back of work, insert RH needle between 1st and 2nd sts on LH needle and draw yo through to front, K next st, pass yo over K st.

⊠ RT: With tip of RH needle, sl yo off LH needle K-wise, K next st, pass yo over K st.

ⱴ On WS (when working flat): With yarn forward, Sl1 p-wise, take yarn to back over top of needle. On RS (when working in the round): Take yarn to back of work between the needles then bace over the needle to the front and then the back between the needles, slip the next st p-wise.
Knit into the row below.

b Knit into the row below.

⟋ C3: With yarn back, slip next stitch, K2, psso the 2 knit sts.

8 STEEKING

Cutting your knitting sounds scary, but it's a great technique for colourwork as it means you can knit in the round, always viewing the right side of your knitting.

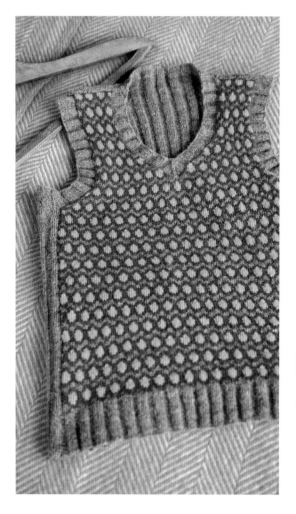

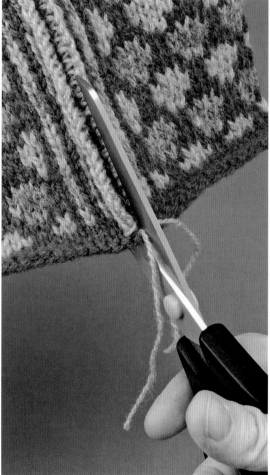

STEEKING WITHOUT FEAR
Jane Crowfoot

When creating colourwork garments, it is easier to ensure the patterning is correct when you're looking at the right side of the work while knitting. In order to avoid having to work wrong-side rows, knitters have developed a technique to allow you to knit an entire garment in the round. This means that you only ever look at the right side of the work, and for stocking stitch patterns, you only need to knit and not purl.

Armholes, neck holes and even cardigan openings are then created after the tube of knitting is complete, by cutting openings. These openings are knitted as bridges of stitches called steeks. These areas are waste fabric, which will be cut and then folded back to create a facing.

The steek is cut through with a sharp pair of scissors once the knitted piece is cast off, or the stitches are held on holders or waste yarn. Cutting your knitting can be daunting, but there are a couple of things that will help ease the anxiety of putting scissors through your knitted piece.

Making the right decisions

If you have never knitted or cut through a steek, then it's logical to have a little practice on some swatches before launching into cutting through a complicated (and perhaps expensive) knitted project.

Try knitting up a few samples – these don't have to be knitted in the round, and do not have to include colourwork as in our sample, although a swatch close to your intended project will give you more confidence.

The most important decision you make is your choice of yarn. In order to hold the stitches and not unravel as you cut, it is best for beginners to choose a 'sticky' yarn that holds onto the knitted stitches. A great choice is something like a 100% Shetland wool, or something with a proportion of 'hairy' or 'fluffy' yarn such as mohair, cashmere or angora. The hairs on the yarn enable the stitches to 'stick' together rather like Velcro.

Obviously, a slippery yarn such as bamboo or silk would not be a good choice for your first cut!

The steek

It is essential that you make the steek wide enough in order to be able to cut and pick up a new edge. Make sure that you have allowed enough stitches to have a central stitch through which you will cut, and have a pair of complete stitches either side of the central stitch.

Thus you could choose to have a central steek made up from as little as 5 stitches. However, in order to err on the side of caution, I would recommend one of 7 or 9 stitches **(1)**.

Using a sewn stitch to stabilise the steek

Although it is possible to stabilise the steek using hand-sewn stitches, it is preferable to use your sewing machine to do so before you start to cut. Many knitters have different opinions on the best stitch to use to do this, but the key is to use a stitch and a speed which will not stretch your knitted fabric **(2, below)**.

A zig-zag stitch may be a good idea as this does not inhibit the elasticity of the knitted piece as much as a straight stitch. The stitch length needs to be short enough that you are piercing each row of knitting, and therefore every strand of yarn. It is usually best to use a coordinating thread colour, although the sample shown here uses a contrast thread to make it visible.

If you have not done a Fair Isle design then it is a good idea to use a hand-sewn running stitch in a contrast thread to mark the central stitch – this means you are less likely to sew in a wonky line. Using your preferred stitch, sew a line of stitches down the centre of each stitch to either side of the central stitch, making sure you do a little reverse sewing at either end to make sure the stitches will not unravel.

Adding a crochet edging to stabilise the edge

An alternative (or extra) method for securing your cut edge is to add a double crochet (US single crochet) edge.

This is a relatively easy technique, but you do need to be able to identify the two different sides of a stitch. One complete stitch creates a 'V' shape. Half of one stitch and half of another when sitting next to each other creates a tent or triangular shape. To work this crochet edge, you need to work along one side of the central stitch and one side of the stitch either to the left or the right of it.

Choose a crochet hook smaller in diameter than the knitting needle you used to knit the fabric. (We have knitted on 4mm and picked up with a 3mm hook.)

1   Fold your knitted piece so that you can clearly see the sides of the 2 stitches that you need to pick up.

2   Insert the hook through so that you have picked up the right side of 1 stitch and the left side of the central stitch.

3   Wrap the yarn around the hook and draw through to create 1 loop of yarn on the hook.

4   Wrap the yarn around the hook again to create 1 chain.

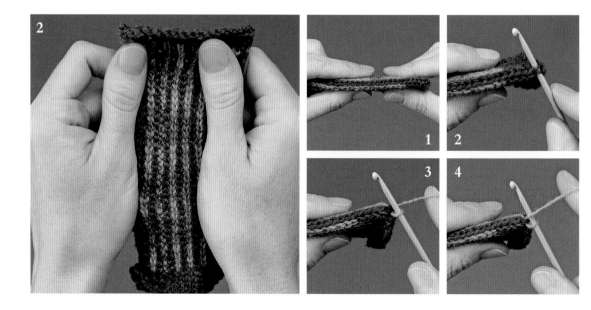

5   Insert the hook through the next 'pair' of stitches along.

6   Wrap the yarn around the hook and draw through the stitches to create a yarn loop on the hook. There are now 2 stitches on the crochet hook.

7   Wrap the yarn around the hook again and draw this yarn through both loops on the hook with the crochet hook facing down so that it does not catch or split the wrong yarn.

8   Continue in this way, creating a nice, even double crochet edge. When you get to the end, cut the yarn and draw through the final stitch.

9   Turn the work and repeat this process along the opposite side of the central stitch.

10 Once complete, you'll see that you have accounted for the whole of the central stitch and one side of the stitches to the left and to the right of it. If you stretch the fabric gently you should be able to see the 'ladder' that the yarn creates through the middle of the central stitch – this is the line along which you are going to cut.

Cutting the steek

11 Using a pair of sharp scissors, cut along the central line – remember to breathe!

Take the time to look at your cut piece and be, perhaps, surprised at its lack of unravelling. Cut Shetland wool really doesn't go anywhere. In fact, many knitters don't even add any stabilising measures, and simply cut through it. The edge is really very secure.

12 If you used the double crochet edging, you will see that this makes a really neat finish to the edge, which now just needs to be slip stitched to the wrong side of your piece. The edge will now be perfectly secure, and as you wash and wear the item, the slight natural felting will add further strength to the edging.

Once you have cut a swatch, you may be ready to jump straight in to a full-sized garment. If you're still not feeling quite confident enough, try playing around with different yarn types and swatches to build even more confidence, and knowledge of what works best for you.

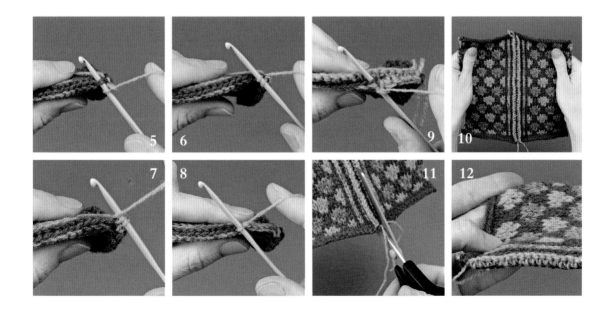

MILNE TANK TOP
Todd Gocken

This smart colourwork tank top for men uses interesting construction, including steeking.

This is a great project if you want to try your hand at steeking. The back is knitted first, although its unusual construction means that it extends around under the arms and contains most of the armhole.

The front is knitted in the round – so that you are always looking at the right side of the colourwork and just knitting – and includes a bridge of stitches called a steek. The finished tube of knitting is then cut open so that it lies flat; the front is actually narrower than the back.

Todd Gocken is an American designer who likes to use interesting textures and patterning in his patterns for men. The colourwork design in his tank top has a vintage look and feel thanks to the subtle colours of Jamieson & Smith's 2ply Jumper Weight wool.

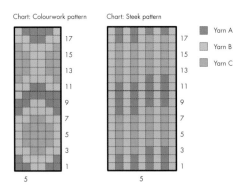

Chart: Colourwork pattern   Chart: Steek pattern

Yarn A
Yarn B
Yarn C

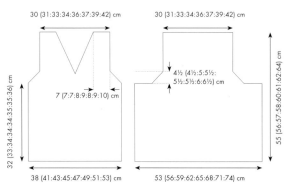

30 (31:33:34:36:37:39:42) cm

30 (31:33:34:36:37:39:42) cm

32 (33:34:34:34:35:35:36) cm

7 (7:7:8:9:8:9:10) cm

4½ (4½:5:5½: 5½:5½:6:6½) cm

55 (56:57:58:60:61:62:64) cm

38 (41:43:45:47:49:51:53) cm

53 (56:59:62:65:68:71:74) cm

SIZE									
To Fit	91	96	101	107	112	117	122	127	cm
Chest	36	38	40	42	44	46	48	50	in
Actual	91	97	102	107	112	117	122	127	cm
Chest	36	38	40	42	44	46	48	50	in
Actual	55	56	57	58	60	61	62	64	cm
Length	21½	22	22½	23	23½	24	24½	25	in

YARN
Jamieson & Smith 2ply Jumper Weight
(Knits as 4ply; 100% Shetland wool; 115m/25g balls)

A shade FC64	5	5	6	6	7	7	7	8	x 25g balls
B shade 118	2	2	3	3	3	3	3	4	x 25g balls
C shade FC45	1	1	2	2	2	2	2	2	x 25g balls

NEEDLES
1 set 3mm (UK 11/US 2) circular needles, 40cm long
1 set 3mm (UK 11/US 2) double-pointed needles
1 set 3.25mm (UK 10/US 3) circular needles, 40cm long
1 pair 3.25mm (UK 10/US 3) needles

TENSION
Back: 30 sts and 40 rows to 10cm over st st
Front: 30 sts and 30 rows to 10cm over Fair Isle pattern

SPECIAL ABBREVIATIONS
mrk: Marker

Back

Using 3.25mm needles and yarn A, cast on 156 (162:174:180:192:204:210:222) sts.
Work in K3, P3 ribbing for 32 (33:34:34:34:35:35:36) cm.

Shape armholes

Cont to work in rib, and cast off
20 (21:24:24:26:30:30:30) sts at beg of next 2 rows.
116 (120:126:132:140:144:150:162) sts.
Dec 2 st at beg of every row for 14 (14:15:16:17:17:18:19)
rows until 88 (92:96:100:106:110:114:124) sts rem.
Work even in rib until armhole meas 22
(23:23:25:25:26:27:28) cm.
Cast off 20 (22:21:23:26:25:27:29) sts at beg of next
2 rows.
Place rem 48(48:54:54:54:60:60:66) sts (for back of neck)
on holder.

Front

Using 3.25mm needles cast on
114 (120:126:132:138:144:150:156) sts.
Work in K3, P3 ribbing for 5cm ending with a WS row.
Switch to 3mm circular needle. Knit first row of
colourwork patt from chart, repeating motif as necessary,
pm, cast 9 sts (steek) onto the end of the needle, pm, and
join in the round.
123 (129:135:141:147:153:159:165) sts.
Work in st st colourwork patt for the Front and vertical
steek patt for the 9 stitches between the markers.
Continue with patt until work measures
32 (33:34:34:34:35:35:36) cm from cast-on edge.

Shape armholes

Next rnd: P1, SSK, work in colourwork patt to last three
sts before mrk, K2tog, P1, slm, work to end of round as set.
Rep this round 13 (13:14:15:16:16:17:18) more times,
switching to 3mm DPNs when the circumference becomes
too small to work comfortably on the circular needles.
95 (101:105:109:113:119:123:127) sts.

Neck shaping

Next rnd: P1, patt 42 (45:47:49:51:54:56:58) sts, pm (this
marks the centre), patt 42 (45:47:49:51:54:56:58) sts, P1,
slm, work to end of round.
Next rnd: P1, work in colourwork patt to 2 sts before
centre mrk, K2tog, slm, SSK, work in patt to 1 st before
mrk, P1, slm, work to end of round.
93 (99:103:107:111:117:121:125) sts.
Next rnd: P1, work in patt to 3 sts before centre mrk,
K2tog, P1, slm, cast on 9 sts (neck steek), pm, P1, SSK, work
in patt to 1 st before mrk, P1, slm, work to end of rnd.
Next rnd: P1, work in patt to 3 sts before mrk, K2tog, P1,
slm, work neck steek as other steek, slm, P1, SSK, work in

patt to 1 st before mrk, P1, slm, work to end of rnd.
Rep last round 21 (22:25:25:24:28:28:28) more times.
58 (62:60:64:70:68:72:76) sts (inc steeks).
Cont working without decreases until armhole measures
22 (23:23:25:25:26:27:28) cm. Cast off.

Cutting the steeks

Add a stabilising measure, such as sewn stitches or a crochet
edging, if you wish. Carefully cut along centre stitch of
steeks, fold over and secure to back of work. For more
information about steeking, see our Masterclass on page 110.

Finishing

Block Front and Back to measurements. Sew Fronts to
Back along shoulder seams. Sew side seams.

Neckband

With RS of work facing, starting at the back right
shoulder seam, work 48 (48:54:54:54:60:60:66) sts from
back neck (matching the K3, P3 ribbing), pick up and knit
51 (51:57:57:57:63:63:63) sts along the column of purl sts
from the Left Front, M1 at centre front, then pick up and
knit 51 (51:57:57:57:63:63:63) sts along the purl sts on the
Right Front.
150 (150:168:168:168:186:186:192) sts.

Join to work in the round.
Continue to work in K3, P3 ribbing until 1 st before
centre front st, Sl 2tog, K1, p2sso, work in K3, P3 ribbing
to end of round.
Repeat this round until ribbing measures 2.5cm.
Cast off loosely.

Armbands

With RS of work facing, pick up and knit
150 (156:162:174:174:186:192:198) sts along armhole
edge between side seams by picking up 1 st for every
armhole cast off st and 1 for every row (these will be
the purl sts on the Front).
Work in K3, P3 ribbing for 2.5cm.
Cast off loosely.
Weave in all loose ends.

SLIP STITCH COLOURWORK

9

Explore the use of slip stitch methods to create colourful effects in your knitting without having to knit with more than one colour per row.

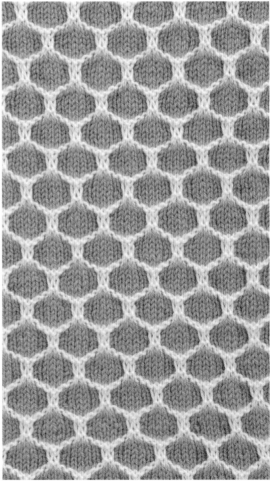

PLAYING WITH COLOUR
Emma King

A slip stitch in knitting is created by doing exactly what the name suggests: a stitch is slipped from the left needle to the right without doing anything to it. Therefore, it hasn't been worked, but it has moved from one needle to the other, which is where it would have ended up even if it had been worked. So, progress has been made across the row, but that particular stitch will not have had any height added to it. It is important to note that in most cases the stitch will be slipped purlwise. This is so that the stitch doesn't become twisted.

Creating different effects

Slip stitches are used in many different ways – for example, in shaping, to create an edge or to place a bead. Here, though, we are focusing on using slip stitches to create effective multicoloured patterns.

We will be looking at how to create Fair Isle effects, a 3D effect and a mosaic, and how to use slip stitches to blend colours. You will also see that understanding what a slip stitch can do will help you use it to full effect in your own designs.

First of all, let's look at what a slip stitch can do when worked in just one colour **(1)**. The swatch shown here is created using a simple slip stitch pattern in a single colour as follows:

Row 1: K1, (yfwd, Sl 1, ybck, K1) to end.
Row 2: Purl.
Row 3: K2, (yfwd, Sl 1, ybck, K1) to last 3 sts, yfwd, Sl 1, ybck, K2.
Row 4: Purl.

On row 1, every other stitch is slipped and the yarn is brought to the front first, then taken to the back again after the stitch has been slipped. This creates little 'bars' of yarn on the front of the work. Row 3 is the same, except the row starts with a 'K2' so that the slip stitches sit in between the bars of row 1.

This creates a lovely woven-like texture. It is also a very firm, flat fabric. But if we really want to bring this stitch pattern to life, just look at what the introduction of a second colour can do **(2)**. This is simply rows 1 and 2 worked in pink and rows 3 and 4 worked in purple. The result is a stunning two-colour piece of knitting which

appears complicated and yet it is actually very simple.

An effective variation of this stitch is to work the same 4-row pattern, but this time carrying the 'bars' of yarn across the wrong side of the work. The result is extremely Fair Isle-like.

Colourwork such as Fair Isle would of course require you to work with more than one colour across each row, but here you are only ever using one colour per row – instead you are just making it appear as if more than one colour has been used. The result is an effective multicoloured design without the usual effort! This can be said for all the multicoloured slip stitch patterns that we will be exploring here.

To be able to use slip stitch patterns in multi-coloured designs to full effect, it is important that we understand how it works. Let's take a closer look at the construction of two more swatches.

In swatch **3**, rows 1 and 2 have been worked in pink, but when row 3 is worked in purple, the slip stitches all remain the pink colour of the previous row.

This is because, as discussed previously, they haven't actually been worked and therefore haven't become purple and instead have remained pink. This means that when viewing row 3 on the needle, it looks like every other stitch is pink even though purple was used to work the row – a clever illusion!

This can be taken a step further by introducing a third colour and playing with the number of worked stitches/ slipped stitches and whether the yarn is held at the front or the back **(4)**. The swatch shown here uses three colours and every fourth stitch (on the right side) is slipped.

3D effects

Slip stitch patterns are often used to frame areas of colour. The Abella cushion design on page 120 uses a slip stitch pattern that creates a honeycomb effect as shown in this swatch **(5)**. The blue hexagons are framed by a trellis of turquoise. What appears quite complicated is again quite simply achieved. It is essentially 2 rows of turquoise, 6 rows of blue, 2 rows of turquoise, 6 rows of blue and so on, as shown in swatch **6**.

However, the vertical of the trellis has been created by constantly slipping 2 turquoise stitches when the 6 rows of blue are being worked. These 2 stitches are only worked on the 2 rows of turquoise. This causes the 2 turquoise stitches to be stretched, as they are essentially being pulled up 6 rows so the stitches appear elongated. The 6 rows of blue are creating a solid fabric behind them and so a 3D effect is also created.

The further a slip stitch is stretched, the more elongated it will appear and the knock-on effect of this is that the 3D effect is further enhanced due to the fabric being pulled more.

It is worth noting that the 'bars' of yarn have been kept on the wrong side throughout, so they do not feature.

We have worked the swatch again, but this time we have reversed the stocking stitch of the hexagons, and rather than working the trellis in garter stitch as in the previous swatch, we have worked it in stocking stitch **(7)**.

This change in stitch use has allowed us to create quite a different effect while still using the same basic slip stitch pattern. Consider playing with slip stitch patterns by experimenting with the type of stitch you work the pattern over.

Mosaic patterns

Another popular use of slip stitches is to create mosaic patterns. Again, the mosaic pattern relies on the knitter creating the illusion that more than one colour has been used within a row, when in actual fact – just like the swatches we have already looked at – it is just a stripe sequence again.

In the swatch shown here **(8)**, a 12-row pattern repeat has been worked and the stripe pattern is 2 rows of turquoise, 2 of cream, 2 of turquoise and so on. Slip stitches feature on both the right-side and wrong-side rows with the yarn always held on the wrong side so that the 'bars' don't interfere with the stocking stitch appearance.

Slipping stitches on both sides of the work is often used in mosaic patterns to achieve the desired shapes. It is this clever planning of the position of the slipped stitches in relation to the worked stitches that creates the mosaic effect.

Blending

One of our favourite effects with slip stitches is creating soft transitions from one colour to the next when doing something as simple as stripes.

For example, this swatch **(9)** shows three different blues worked in a stripe pattern – each coloured stripe is 4 rows deep.

But a completely different effect can be created using the same stripe sequence **(10)**. This time, the first row of each stripe has been worked by slipping every other stitch with the yarn at the front and then at the back for each knit stitch – i.e. 'bars' on the right side of the work.

This is the same as the first row of the pink/purple swatch (number **2**), but here the technique has been used to create an optical illusion. The fact that the two colours share the first row of the stripe softens the move from one colour to the next and this creates a 'blurred' effect which is enhanced by carrying the 'bars' on the right side. It is an effective way of making colours appear to blend in and out of each other. Perhaps consider using a textured yarn to enhance this further.

Creating your own designs

When using slip stitches in your own designs, consider the following:

Will tension be affected?

Introducing a slip stitch to a pattern will most certainly alter the tension. It will have most impact on the row tension, but the stitch tension will be affected, too. The row tension changes considerably because, as we have learned, each time a stitch is slipped it fails to grow in height.

Therefore, the more rows it is slipped, the more your row tension will be affected. The impact on stitch tension is slightly less due to the fact that the width of the stitch is ever-present, but the fact that it's being slipped rather than worked means that it won't maintain the width that it would normally.

Do you want to create a 3D effect or a flatter fabric?

The 3D effect that we explored in the honeycomb pattern was created by slipping the same stitches (with the 'bars' at the back) several times. The more you continue to slip the same stitch(es), the greater the 3D effect. If you wanted to do the opposite and create a flatter fabric, alternating the position of the slipped stitches (with the 'bars' at the front) will achieve this, as shown in the pink and pink/purple swatches on page 117.

Finally, make time to experiment!

There is great fun to be had from experimenting with slip stitch patterns. What we have discussed here will hopefully have given you a feel for how slip stitches work and what they can do, but we have only scratched the surface - we would certainly recommend that you now have a play! The possibilities are endless – not just the potential for the slip stitches themselves, but also with the yarns that you choose to use, and the stitch that you choose to work them over.

Look at the four-colour swatch here **(11)**. It is an 8-row stripe – 2 rows of turquoise, 2 of purple, 2 of pink and 2 of cream. We have slipped every fourth stitch of the turquoise for the duration of the next 4 rows. We have then continued with the stripe pattern, but have slipped the cream, then the pink, then the purple and so on. However, we could have worked it in fewer colours or more colours; slipped fewer stitches or more stitches; used two different-textured yarns… see what we mean? Endless possibilities!

ABELLA CUSHION
Emma King

Use slip stitch patterning to produce a lovely honeycomb-like design.

Playing with slip stitch patterning can create interesting three-dimensional effects, such as this honeycomb design used by Emma King on her Abella cushion.

'The repetition and layering often found in nature was the inspiration for this design,' says Emma. 'The simple slip stitch pattern creates the illusion of two layers of knitting while casting a shadow on the "underneath" layer.'

The patterning appears on the front panel of the cushion; the reverse is made up of two stocking stitch panels, joined using ribbed button bands with pearly buttons.

Emma has knitted her cushion in Bergère de France Sport, a great-value blend of wool and acrylic. She has picked two neutral shades to ensure the cushion complements most home décor schemes, but the yarn is available in a wide range of brighter colours too, if you'd prefer a more vibrant result.

To find out more about creating different effects using slip stitch patterning, take a look at our detailed Masterclass, starting on page 114.

SIZE
40cm x 40cm (16in x 16in)

YARN
Bergère de France Sport (Heavy DK weight; 51% wool, 49% acrylic; 90m/50g balls)
A Laurier (20711) 4 x 50g balls
B Natural (27166) 2 x 50g balls

NEEDLES & ACCESSORIES
1 pair 4mm (UK 8/US 6) knitting needles
Cushion pad, 40cm x 40cm
7 x 20mm buttons

TENSION
20 sts and 27 rows to 10cm over st st using 4mm needles

Front panel

Using 4mm needled and yarn B cast on 84 sts.
Row 1 (RS): Knit.
Row 2: Knit.

Change to yarn A.
Row 3: K1, Sl 2, (K6, Sl 2) to last st, K1.
Row 4: P1, Sl 2, (P6, Sl 2) to last st, P1.
Repeat rows 3 and 4 twice more.

Change to yarn B.
Row 9: Knit.
Row 10: Knit.

Change to yarn A.
Row 11: K5, Sl 2, (K6, Sl 2) to last 5 sts, K5.
Row 12: P5, Sl 2, (P6, Sl 2) to last 5 sts, P5.
Repeat rows 11 and 12 twice more.
Repeat the last 16 rows eight more times.

Change to yarn B.
Next row: Knit.
Next row: Knit.
Cast off.

Back

Lower section
Using 4mm needles and yarn A cast on 81 sts.
Row 1 (RS): Knit.
Row 2: Purl.
Repeat last 2 rows until work meas 27cm from cast-on edge, ending with a WS row.

Change to yarn B.
Next row: Knit.
Next row: P3, (K3, P3) to end.
Next row: K3, (P3, K3) to end.
Repeat last 2 rows 4 more times, ending with a RS row.
Cast off in pattern.

Upper section
Using 4mm needles and yarn B cast on 81 sts.
Row 1 (RS): K3, (P3, K3) to end.
Row 2: P3, (K3, P3) to end.
Repeat last 2 rows once more, ending with a WS row.
Next row: K3, (cast off 3 sts, K3, P3, K3) to last 6 sts, cast off 3 sts, K3.

Next row: P3, (turn, cast on 3 sts, turn, P3, K3, P3) to last 6 sts, turn, cast on 3 sts, turn, P3.
Next row: K3, (P3, K3) to end.
Next row: P3, (K3, P3) to end.

Change to yarn A.
Next row: Knit.
Next row: Purl.
Repeat last 2 rows until work meas 13cm from cast-on edge, ending with a WS row.
Cast off.

Making up

Block pieces gently to measurements, following any yarn care instructions on the ball band.
Sew the cast-on edge of the front to the cast-on edge of the lower back. Sew the side seams.
Sew the cast-off edge of the upper back to the cast-off edge of the front. Sew the side seams, leaving the edges open at each end of the buttonhole flap.
Lining the buttons up with the buttonholes, stitch them into place on the rib of the lower section.
Insert cushion pad and fasten buttons.

10 REVERSIBLE KNITS

Try your hand at this fascinating technique in which both sides of your knitting look alike, but with reversed colours. It's perfect for garments such as scarves where both sides of the knitting can be seen.

REVERSIBLE DOUBLE KNITTING
Jane Crowfoot

Double knitting is a technique that has two main uses. The first is for creating tubes of fabric using straight knitting needles, and is particularly useful for glove fingers and pockets. The second is used in the Cuthbert Scarf and Hat set on page 126, and makes a flat piece of knitting which is reversible. It has two sides showing images that may be thought of as a 'positive' and a 'negative'.

If you have never tried this technique before then it may be a good idea to have a go at producing a reversible stocking stitch sampler in two colours first, then once you are comfortable with the method you can progress to following more complex patterns and charts. The Cuthbert Scarf and Hat set also includes a section of runes where the writing is not a simple reverse on the second side, adding extra knitting interest.

Casting on

To create a reversible fabric you will need to cast on enough stitches to produce both sides of the knitted piece. If you want 20 stitches on either side, you will need to cast on a total of 40 stitches. To keep an open base to the knitted tube, cast on using the backwards loop method and alternate between the two colours as follows:

1 Make a slip knot using both yarns, then hold the yarns over your thumb and first finger.

2 Bring needle over yarn A on thumb and pick up loop.

3 Take needle over yarn B on first finger and pick up a loop.

4 Continue to work steps 2 and 3 until you have the required number of stitches. You will see that yarn A, which was held over the thumb, lies at the front, with yarn B forming a cast on edge behind this.

To create a closed edge at the bottom of the piece, simply cast on half of the total number of stitches and work into front and back of each stitch in the first row.

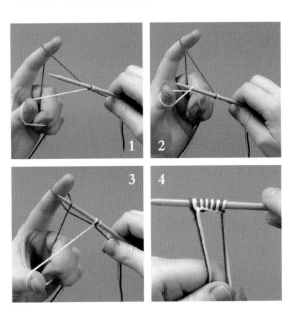

Working a reverse stocking stitch tube

This is the easiest double knitting technique to start with. Using two different coloured yarns allows you to see clearly which stitches belong to which side, and no moving of yarns is needed.

1 Prepare to purl the first stitch, using yarn B as this is the colour of the first stitch, bringing the second colour (A) over your working yarn, to keep the sides of the tube closed.

2 Purl the first stitch as normal using yarn B.

3 Leaving yarn B at the front, knit the second stitch using yarn A.

4 Continue to work alternate stitches using yarn B for purling the front layer and yarn A for knitting the back layer. When you have finished the row you will work the next row purling the front stitches with yarn A and knitting with yarn B. After a few rows you should be able to see that you are making a tube with reverse stocking stitch on the outside.

Stocking stitch tube

This time, the stitches on the layer facing you will be worked with a knit stitch, and the reverse stitches will be purled.

As before, cross the reverse yarn over the front yarn before working the first stitch. This ensures that the sides of your tube are closed.

1 Knit the first stitch using the correct colour – in this case, B.

2 Bring both yarns forward between the knitting needles.

3 Purl the next stitch using the reverse colour (A).

4 Take both yarns back between the knitting needles. Knit the next stitch using the original colour.

As before, when you work the following row you will be using the opposite colour to work the knit stitches as you now have the opposite colour fabric facing you.

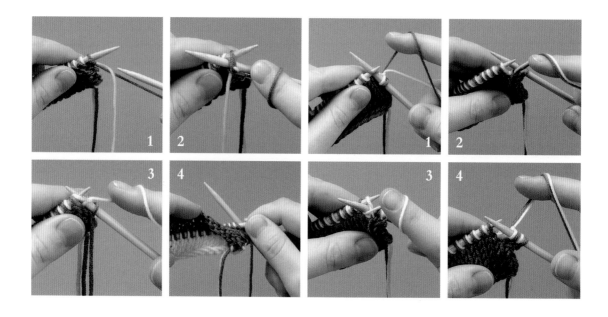

Working a reversible pattern from a chart

Each square on the chart (below right) represents 2 stitches – one on side A of the fabric (RS) and one on side B, the reverse side. For the rope motif on the chart a dark shaded square represents dark grey on the right side and light grey on the reverse side of the work. The lighter square represents light grey on the right side and dark grey on the reverse side.

1   Stitch 7 of row 16 is being worked using pale grey yarn with a knit stitch.

2   Both yarns are brought forward to work the reverse stitch, which is purled using dark grey.

3+4   The next stitch from the chart is 8 and appears on the chart as dark grey, thus the front stitch is knitted using dark grey and then the reverse stitch is purled using the lighter colour.

As before, when you work the reverse side row you will need to work the opposite colours for knit and purl stitches. It is a good idea to mark an arrow at the side of the rows to remind yourself which direction you should be following the chart and which colour to knit and purl with.

Keeping your tension

It is common that the tension of your piece will be slightly looser than normal. This is because the yarn is used on every alternate stitch and is thus stranded across a stitch between use each time. If you find that your tension is really loose then you may want to try using a slightly smaller needle.

Casting off

To work a closed cast off, treat both the front stitch and the reverse stitch as one and cast them off together, thus knitting into 2 stitches each time.

To keep the tube open, you will need to separate the two sets of stitches by slipping alternate stitches onto different needles. They can then be cast off separately.

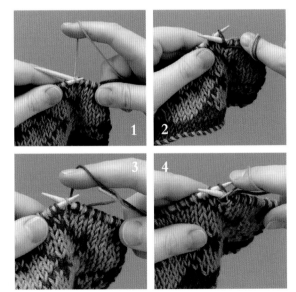

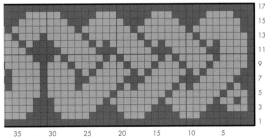

CUTHBERT SCARF & HAT
Judy Furlong

Keep out the winter chill in this unisex, reversible Fair Isle set inspired by ancient runes and stone carvings.

This set has been designed by Judy Furlong, and was inspired by Celtic and Viking stone carvings such as those found in Orkney. The rope and Celtic knot are common motifs, and the triskele, dating from the Bronze Age, represents the spiral of life and the interaction between land, sea and sky. The runes – principally Norwegian Futhark – are an ancient form of writing and spell out *The Knitter* on the scarf and 'Runes' on the hat. The stick nature of this writing lends itself to Fair Isle designs and gives a chance to use a slightly more complicated type of double knitting, where the pattern differs on the two sides.

Says Judy, 'The scarf is knitted in two parts and joined by grafting in approximately the centre so that the writing is the right way up at both ends. Make the scarf as long as you like, but just decide first what the midpoint will be to make sure that the repeats work out. The hat has a provisional cast-on edge for a rounded, soft finish that allows elastic to be inserted, and ensures a firm fit for the recipient of this cosy set.'

If you haven't tried double knitting before, see our Masterclass on page 122.

Reading charts

Charts are read from right to left on Side A facing rows and from left to right on Side B facing rows.

All charts except Scarf Chart 2 are drawn showing Side A only. When Side A faces you, Side A sts are knitted in the colour shown on the chart, and Side B sts are purled using the opposite colour. When Side B faces, Side B sts are knitted and A are purled, and the chart is read from left to right. Stocking stitch fabric should be maintained on both sides. Side B sts are not shown on the chart.

Scarf Chart 2 is drawn showing both sides at once and is worked in exactly the same way, except that both Side A and Side B sts are written out on the chart. This is necessary because in order for the writing to read correctly, the lettering has to run in the opposite direction on the reverse side. To read this chart, when Side A faces you, knit the Side A sts in the colour shown then purl the Side B sts in the colour shown on the chart – this may or may not be the second colour. When Side B faces, Side B sts are knitted and A are purled, and the chart is read from left to right.

SCARF SIZE

191cm (75in) long (adjustable) x 28cm (11in) wide

YARN FOR SCARF & HAT

Stylecraft Pure Luxury Merino DK (100% merino wool; 119m/50g balls)
A Slate (3638) 4 x 50g balls
B Flint (3641) 3 x 50g balls
C Ivory (3631) 3 x 50g balls
D Truffle (3633) 4 x 50g balls
E Cafe (3640) 2 x 50g balls
F Ink (3642) 4 x 50g balls

NEEDLES & ACCESSORIES

1 pair 4mm (UK 8/US 6) knitting needles
3–3.5mm (UK 11–9/US D3–E4) crochet hook
Spare needles or waste yarn

TENSION

22 sts and 30 rows to 10cm over double knitting (reversible st st) using 4mm needles, after pressing or light steaming

PATTERN NOTES

The scarf and hat are reversible but to simplify the instructions the two sides are referred to as Side A and Side B

Scarf

Part 1

Using 4mm needles and yarn A, cast on 122 sts.
Join in yarn B and work charts as foll, using the double knitting technique:

1st sequence: Scarf Chart 1 (Rope), Scarf Chart 2 (Runes), Scarf Chart 1 upside down, Scarf Chart 3 (Celtic knot).

2nd sequence: Scarf Chart 1 (Rope), Scarf Chart 2 (Runes), Scarf Chart 1 upside down, Scarf Chart 4 (Triskele).

3rd sequence: As for 1st sequence.

Note that since all charts have an odd number of rows, the first row of Scarf Charts 2, 3 and 4 will be read from left to right.

Slip the sts onto 2 spare needles or length of yarn separating the two sides ready for grafting as foll:

Slip the first st onto needle 1, the 2nd onto needle 2, 3rd onto needle 1, 4th onto needle 2. Continue as established until all sts have been slipped and the two sides are held on separate needles.

Scarf chart 1

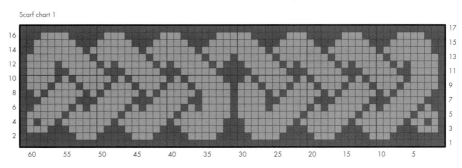

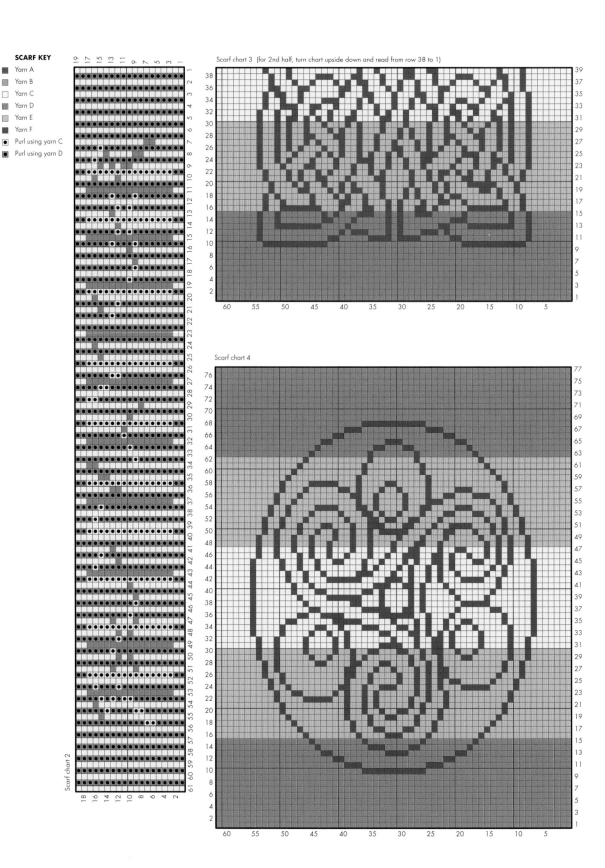

SCARF KEY

- Yarn A
- Yarn B
- Yarn C
- Yarn D
- Yarn E
- Yarn F
- Purl using yarn C
- Purl using yarn D

Scarf chart 2

Scarf chart 3 (for 2nd half, turn chart upside down and read from row 38 to 1)

Scarf chart 4

Part 2

Using 4mm needles and yarn A, cast on 122 sts.
Join in yarn B and work 2nd sequence as given for Part 1, followed by 1st sequence ending with row 76 of Scarf Chart 3 (Celtic Knot). Row 77 will be used to graft the two ends together. Separate the two sides by slipping them onto two needles as for Part 1.

Making up

Joining both parts together

Weave in any loose ends.
Graft the two parts together, one side at a time using the background colours for Celtic Knot: yarn D for Side A and yarn F for Side B.

Double fringe

Cut 122 lengths of yarn approximately 40cm long in each of yarn A (for Side A) and yarn B (for side B).
Starting at one end with Side B uppermost, insert crochet hook from side to side underneath the 1st stitch of the first row knitted in yarn B. Fold a length of yarn (yarn B) in half, place over the crochet hook and draw the loop through. Slip the cut ends through the loop and draw up to make a knot. Repeat along the width of the scarf. Repeat on Side A using yarn A. Repeat for the other end. Trim fringe to desired length.

Hat

As you are working in the round, Side A is always facing and charts are read from right to left.
Using 4mm double-pointed needles and waste yarn, cast on 136 sts.
Join and mark the end of the rnd, change to yarn B and knit 2 rounds. Join in yarn A (do not break off yarn B) and knit 2 rounds.

Making hem

(also used for elastic casing)
★K1 in yarn A from the needle, P1 in yarn B from the provisional cast-on edge, repeat from ★ until the last st on the needle, K1 in yarn A. Cast on 1 st in yarn B. 272 sts. The cast on st is necessary because there is usually one less st available to pick up than the number provisionally cast on. Remove waste yarn.

HAT SIZE
To fit average-sized adult's head
Head circumference 57–61cm (22½–24in)
Crown to brim 21½cm (8½in)

YARN FOR HAT ONLY
Stylecraft Pure Luxury Merino DK (100% merino wool; 119m/50g balls)
A Slate (3638) 1 x 50g ball
B Flint (3641) 1 x 50g ball
C Ivory (3631) 1 x 50g ball
D Truffle (3633) 1 x 50g ball
E Cafe (3640) 1 x 50g ball
F Ink (3642) 1 x 50g ball

NEEDLES & ACCESSORIES
1 set 4mm (UK 8/US 6) double-pointed needles (DPNs)
Cable needle (cn), stitch markers
Waste yarn, 2 blunt tapestry needles
Bodkin needle and approx 65cm x 5mm (25½in x ¼in) elastic (optional)

TENSION
22 sts and 30 rows to 10cm over double knitting (reversible st st) using 4mm needles, after pressing or light steaming

PATTERN & CHART NOTES
See Scarf information

SPECIAL ABBREVIATIONS
K1C: Knit 1 st using yarn C
P1D: Purl 1 st using D
P1F: Purl 1 sts using yarn F
Dec 1 left DK: Decrease 1 st with a left slope in double knitting as follows – First, reorder the sts: slip next st onto RH needle, following st (a purl st) onto cn and hold at back of work, next st onto RH needle, return st from cn to LH needle, then return 2 sts slipped to RH needle back to LH needle. There will now be two 'Side A' sts together followed by two 'Side B' sts together on LH needle. Second, decrease: Sl 1, K1, psso, P2tog.
Dec 1 right DK: Decrease 1 st with a right slope in double knitting as follows – First, reorder the sts: as for Dec 1 left DK. Second, decrease: K2tog, P2tog tbl.

Rope border

Rnd 1: Work the 8 sts (16 sts in total as double knitting) of Hat Chart 1 (Rope) repeating motif 17 times in each round.

Rnds 2–17: Continue until all 17 rnds of Hat Chart 1 are complete.

Runes border

Rnd 1: ★Work the 45 sts (90 sts in total as double knitting) of Hat Chart 2 (Runes), pm, repeat from ★ twice more to end of rnd.

Rnds 2–15: Continue with Hat Chart 2 until rnd 15 has been completed, slipping markers. Dec 2 sts in last round of Runes border.

Shape top runes

Rnd 16 (1st dec rnd): ★K1C, P1D as established, 'Dec 1 left DK', (Tip: Work the first 2 sts in yarn C and the second 2 in yarn D as for st 3 in the chart, the next st is st 4 which is K1C, P1D), pattern to st 43, 'Dec 1 right DK', pattern to marker; rep from the ★ twice more.

Rnd 17: As Hat Chart 2 remembering to omit sts 2 and 44.

Rnd 18: Dec 2 sts in each of the three sections as for Rnd 16.

Rnd 19: As Hat Chart 2 remembering to omit sts 2, 3, 43 and 44.

Shape top triskele

Work from Hat Chart 3, decreasing as set previously, on rnd 1 and the next 8 alternate rnds until 11 decreases have been completed.

Rnds 19–27: Continue following Hat Chart 3 decreasing on this and the next 8 rnds. 30 sts in total.

Rnd 28: K1C (st 1 Side A), P1F (st 1 Side B), ★Sl 1 onto RH needle, slip next st (Side B st) onto cable needle, hold at back of work, repeat from ★, Sl 1 onto RH needle, return Side B sts from cable needle to LH needle, then Side A sts from RH needle to LH needle. In yarn C, Sl 1,

K2tog, psso, in yarn F, P3tog, K1C (st 44 Side A), P1F (st 44 Side B). Repeat from beginning of rnd twice more. 18 sts in total.

Rnd 29: Break off yarns leaving a length for fastening off. Thread two tapestry needles, one in each colour. Slip the first st (Side A) onto yarn C, then the second st (Side B) onto yarn F. Repeat until all sts have been slipped onto yarn. Fasten off taking care not the let the sts show on the reverse side.

Making up

Weave in loose ends except for cast-on edge.

Optional: With a bodkin needle, carefully insert elastic at the cast-on edge, adjust to fit allowing 1cm overlap. Overlap ends and sew together firmly. Slip into fabric and finish off with the remaining loose ends of yarn.

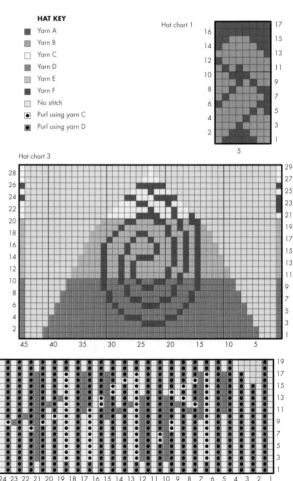

HAT KEY
- Yarn A
- Yarn B
- Yarn C
- Yarn D
- Yarn E
- Yarn F
- No stitch
- Purl using yarn C
- Purl using yarn D

11 STRIPES IN THE ROUND

Develop your techniques for striping colourwork with this easy-to-follow
guide to knitting stripes without a step in sight.

CREATING SEAMLESS COLOUR CHANGES
Jane Crowfoot

Whether you're a whizz at working in the round or if you're just starting out on your adventures with double-pointed or circular needles, learning how to work jogless stripes will help you perfect your technique.

When working on straight needles (thus not in the round), as you reach the end of the row, the working yarn is pulled up along the side of your knitting to work the subsequent row. When working in the round, instead of having definite row starts and finishes, the knitting is worked in a spiral. The last stitch of one round sits next to the first stitch of the next round on every row, right until the end of the piece.

When working in one colour, the point where rows merge is not detectable, but when working stripes – be they wide or narrow – the point where the colour changes between rows becomes recognisable by way of a step or 'jog' in the colour flow. This masterclass aims to show you how to eliminate these jogs and achieve neat stripes to be proud of.

Jogless stripes

In working rows of stripes that are made from more than 2 rows, you can achieve a neat effect by using a slip stitch at the start of the second round of a new colour.

1   This sample shows stripes worked in the usual way on the bottom half – note the step at the change in round. On the upper half, the jogless stripe method has been used to reduce the step.

Cast on your required number of stitches and divide evenly between your needles. Work the first stripe repeat using your chosen colour. (In our sample we have done 4 rows of each colour.) If it helps, use a stitch marker to indicate the start of the next row.

2   ★ Change to the next colour and work 1 complete row making sure that you knit the final stitch of the round.

3   Instead of knitting the next stitch (the first stitch of the next round) slip it purlwise.

4   Carry the yarn across the reverse of the slipped stitch and knit the next stitch. This will pull the stitch up from the row below and will make the appearance of the 'jog' between rows less noticeable (see page 133).

Continue to knit in this colour until you have completed the stripe and repeat from * to end.

Travelling jogless stripes

If you look closely you will see that the first stitch of the round has 1 row fewer than the others. This is only apparent on close scrutiny and will not be obvious to the untrained eye.

However, when this is repeated over a long section, you may find that your work puckers a little because this point has 1 row fewer, and they are stacked on top of each other. If the colour change is moved each round, then this can be spread out, making the change even less noticeable.

To do this you will need to move the colour change along the row by between 1 and 3 stitches; this is referred to as travelling jogless stripes. This method is used in the leg of the Scooter Socks pattern on page 136.

1   Insert a second stitch marker at the place where you wish to change colour on the row before you are due to do so – say 2 or 3 stitches to the left of the last colour change. Shown here by the shoe marker.

* Work up to the stitch marker. Drop the first colour and join in and start working with the new colour.

2   Complete a full round until you reach the new stitch marker. Slip the marker, then instead of knitting the next stitch (the first stitch of the next round) slip it purlwise.

3   Carry the yarn across the reverse of the slipped stitch and knit the next stitch.

Continue in this colour until the penultimate row of the stripe sequence. Insert a stitch marker at the place where you wish to change colour on the next row and repeat from *.

TIP: Do not move any more than 2 or 3 stitches to the left of the previous colour change when planning where to place your marker. You may choose to move over by just 1 stitch, although we've found 2 to be neater. If you move over by too many stitches you may find that you lose track of your row tally and do not fit your desired stripe repeat into the piece.

Spiral or helical stripes

This is a really great technique; the first time we saw it we didn't believe that it could work, and even as we began to see our spiral appear before our eyes, we thought that it was a fluke! Don't be deceived into thinking that this is a complicated technique and don't let images of different balls of yarn attached to the needles at the same time lead you to believe that this method is difficult. It is a relatively simple technique that will leave you with perfect twirling stripes and a feeling of wonder!

4   In this sample, we have used three colours and a set of four DPNs. The bottom half of the sample has been knitted using a traditional technique where the colour is changed at the end of each round, and the top half uses the spiral stripe technique.

Setting up the stitches
Cast on your required number of stitches and divide evenly between your needles.

Work 1 complete row (or more if you need to) in one colour.

5   Knit across all of the stitches on the first DPN using the first colour in the stripe sequence. Drop the yarn at the end of this segment of stitches.

6   Using the second colour in the stripe sequence, knit across all of the stitches on the next DPN. Drop the yarn at the end of this segment of stitches.

7   Finally (if using a total of four DPNs like us), knit across the stitches on the third DPN using the third colour of yarn.

Continuing in the stripe sequence

When working this technique you will be required to change colour at the end of the segment of stitches on the DPN so long as there is a yarn waiting in position ready for you to change colour. When you reach a new yarn at the end of a needle, drop the yarn in use and pick up the new yarn ready for use. You will always pick up the lower of the two yarns if there is more than one waiting for use.

Below is a bit of a strange analogy, but the comparison has helped us to understand this technique.

Imagine that the yarn in use is a bus and that the yarns not being used are passengers waiting at various bus stops. As the bus drives along it picks up the passengers who are waiting, but if there are no passengers to pick up, then the bus does not stop.

OK, so this may be an odd bus because not only does it never let any passengers off, but it also changes colour as it drives along. Still, maybe it will help you to understand what to do!

Can I use different numbers of colours?

In our sample we have used three colours, and the Scooter Socks pattern uses just two colours. Theoretically, you can use this technique to work as many repeated stripe colours as you choose to. However, it is worth making sure that you keep track of your colour order as you can get a bit muddled when using a large number of colours or when working a complicated repeat. And the more colours used, the more the stripes will appear to slope.

If at any time you reach a point where more than one colour appears to be ready for use, then choose the lower colour as this is sure to be the next in the sequence.

When working with lots of colours or when working a complicated stripe sequence it is a really good idea to use stitch markers to help keep track of things.

Avoiding loose or tight stitches at colour changes

When you reach a colour change it is REALLY important that you do not over- or under-tighten the yarn which you are about to use. When knitting in the round the temptation is to pick up and tug at the new yarn in order to avoid a ladder appearing between the stitches. This will cause the stitch to over-tighten and shrink down in size.

Try holding your needles as close together as possible when working the first stitch of the round, pull the yarn gently and only then tighten the stitch once it has been knitted.

TIP: If you want to work wider stripes using the spiral method, you simply need to use more than one ball of that colour. So to work 2-row stripes of blue and white, you will need to have two balls of blue yarn attached one after the other, and two balls of white yarn. One ball of yarn is required for each row of stripe pattern that you desire.

SCOOTER SOCKS

Jen Arnall-Culliford

Knit this lively sock design, with two different striping patterns.

This is the perfect pattern for trying out jogless stripe techniques. Knitting in the round gives a lovely seamless finish to projects, but when you work stripes you get a 'jog' where the colours change. To avoid this there are some clever techniques you can use. This sock pattern allows you to try two of them – travelling jogless stripes in the leg pattern, and helical stripes in the foot. Helical stripes work particularly well on the foot as they avoid any yarn being carried at the WS, which might cause discomfort.

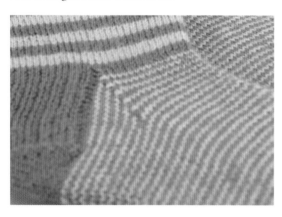

Socks

Cuff

Using 2.5mm double-pointed needles and yarn A, cast on 52 (60:68:76) sts, using yarn A and join to work in the round, taking care not to twist the sts. Place marker for start of round.
Rnd 1: K1 tbl, P1; rep from ★ to end of round.
Repeat last round until cuff meas 3cm.

Ankle

Join in yarn B (but do not break off yarn A; when working stripes yarn not in use can be woven in on alt rows on WS).
Rnd 1: Using yarn B, knit.
Repeat last round 3 more times.
In the next section the original round marker will be left in place, but ignored. A second colour change marker (CCM) will be added and this will be used to mark the start and end of all rounds until the heel. For more guidance on working travelling jogless stripes, see masterclass on p132.
Rnd 5: Using yarn A, knit all stitches to original end of round marker.

SIZE					
	S	M	L	XL	
Unstretched	16	16	21	23	cm
Ankle	6½	7	8½	9	in
Circumference					
Sock Cuff	18	18	23	23	cm
To Floor	7	7	9	9	in

Foot length can be adjusted within the pattern

YARN

Regia 4ply (75% new wool, 25% polyamide; 210m/50g balls)
A Lavandel (1988) 1 x 50g ball
B Hellblau (1945) 1 x 50g ball
Extra yarn may be required for very long feet

NEEDLES & ACCESSORIES

1 set 2.5mm (UK 13–12/ US 1–2) double pointed needles
Stitch holder or waste yarn
2 stitch markers

TENSION

33 sts and 46 rows to 10cm over striped pattern using 2.5mm needles

SPECIAL ABBREVIATIONS

CCM: Colour change marker

PATTERN NOTES

See Masterclass on page 132 for full explanation of travelling jogless stripes and helical stripes. All slipped stitches should be slipped purlwise.

Rnd 6: Using yarn A, Sl 1, knit to end of round marker.

Rnd 7: As round 5.

Rnd 8: Using yarn A, K1, place marker (CCM) to show where colour change will take place, knit to CCM.

Rnd 9: Change to yarn B, K to CCM.

Rnd 10: Using yarn B, Sl 1, knit to CCM.

Rnd 11: Using yarn B, knit to CCM.

Rnd 12: Using yarn B, remove CCM, K1, replace CCM, knit round to CCM.

Rnd 13: Change to yarn A, knit to CCM.

Rnd 14: Using yarn A, Sl 1, knit to CCM.

Rnd 15: Using yarn A, knit to CCM.

Rnd 16: Using yarn A, remove CCM, K1, replace CCM, knit round to CCM.

Continue in stripes as set by rounds 9–16 until sock meas 13 (13:17:17) cm, ending on a round 14 at original start of round marker. Remove CCM.

Heel

Heel flap is worked back and forth in rows, using yarn A only, and is centred on original start of round marker.

Next row: Using yarn A only, K13 (15:17:19), turn.

Next row (WS): ★Sl 1, P1; rep from ★ 12 (14:16:18) more times. You may find it helpful to place 26 (30:34:38) unused instep sts on waste yarn or a holder.

Next row (RS): Sl 1, K25 (29:33:37) sts.

Rep these 2 rows until heel flap is square, ending with a WS row.

Next row: Sl 1, K15 (17:19:21), SSK, K1, turn. 7 (9:11:13) sts remain unworked at the end of this row.

Next row: Sl 1, P7, P2tog, P1, turn. 7 (9:11:13) sts remain unworked at both ends of the row.

Next row: Sl 1, knit until 1 st before gap where last row turned, SSK, K1, turn.

Next row: Sl 1, purl until 1 st before gap where last row turned, P2tog, P1, turn.

Rep last 2 rows until all side sts are consumed, omitting final K1 and P1 on last 2 rows if necessary.

Foot

Resume working in the round as foll:

Using yarn A, knit across heel sts (needle 1). Use an empty needle to pick up 1 st tbl of each slipped stitch on edge of heel flap, this is needle 2, work an additional 2 sts from instep onto this needle.

Use one needle to knit across 22 (26:30:34) instep sts, this is needle 3.

Use a 4th needle to knit last 2 instep sts and pick up 1 st tbl of each slipped stitch on other side of heel flap.

Next rnd: Needle 1 – knit; needle 2 – knit to last 3 sts, SSK, K1; needle 3 – knit; needle 4 – K1, K2tog, knit to end.

Join in yarn B at start of needle 1, but do not use immediately, continue to use yarn A and work needles 1, 2 and 3 as above, working decrease on needle 2.

Pick up yarn B and use it to work needles 1 and 2 as above, working decrease on needle 2.

Return to yarn A and work needles 4 and 1, working decrease on needle 4 as above.

Return to yarn B and work needles 3 and 4, working decrease on needle 4 as above.

Continue to work in yarns A and B, working 2 needles of each and decreasing as set above until you have 52 (60:68:76) sts.

Once the decreases are complete, continue to work 2 needles each of yarns A and B without further shaping until sock meas 3 (3½:4:4½) cm less from heel to needles than desired foot length, ending with yarn B at end of needle 4. Break off yarn B.

From this point on, use yarn A only.

Knit 1 round. Redistribute sts equally over needles so that needle 1 goes from centre of sole of foot to side of foot, needle 2 goes from side of foot to middle of top of foot, needle 3 goes from middle of top foot to side and needle 4 goes from side of foot to middle of sole. Each needle should hold 13 (15:17:19) sts.

Decrease round: Needles 1 & 3 – Knit to last 3 sts, SSK, K1; needles 2 & 4 – K1, K2tog, knit to end. 48 (56:64:72) sts.

Work decreases as set on alternate rounds until 40 sts rem, then work decreases on every round until 16 sts rem.

Needle 1 – knit to end.

Slip all sts purlwise from needle 4 to needle 1. Slip all stitches purlwise from needle 2 to needle 3.

Graft toe stitches together. Weave in all ends.

Wedge stocking stitch toe is finished by grafting toe stitches together, giving a smooth finish. For a tutorial on grafting, see Masterclass 12 on page 138.

Travelling jogless stripes are used in the 4-row stripes, making the colour change hard to spot.

12 KITCHENER STITCH

This invaluable grafting method is used to create invisible seams, and can be used for so much more than socks.

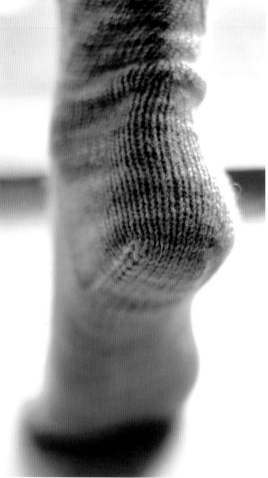

SEAMLESS GRAFTING
Jane Crowfoot

Kitchener stitch or grafting is an amazing technique that every knitter should be familiar with. It allows us to close a set of live stitches seamlessly. The way it weaves the stitches together makes it a thing of joy, but there's much more to this technique than meets the eye and it has many applications; it isn't just for stocking stitch or for the toes of socks. And really, it's not as difficult as it first appears.

In theory, any stitch that you can create on knitting needles can also be grafted. When you perform Kitchener stitch you're re-creating those bumps and Vs that you're so familiar with, only you're re-creating them with a different type of needle. That's all.

It is ideal for shoulder seams (so long as the garment is not too bulky or heavy, where the lack of structure can cause shoulders to sag) and is the best way to deal with the toe end of socks.

At the onset of the First World War, the British secretary of state for war Lord Kitchener rapidly enlisted and trained a vast army. It is his face on the famous 'Your Country Needs You' poster. He also associated himself with a Red Cross plan to encourage British, American and Canadian women to knit various 'comforts' for his troops in the form of hats, gloves, mittens, scarves and socks.

Lord Kitchener is said to have contributed his own sock design to this campaign. The knitted sock patterns of the day used a seam up the toe which could rub uncomfortably against the toes. His design included an invisible grafted toe seam to make the socks more comfortable to wear. This finishing technique later became known as Kitchener stitch.

Working on live stitches

It is a good idea to practise any sewing-up techniques before executing them on a garment or finished knitted piece (perhaps you could try it out on some old tension squares). Kitchener stitch is usually used on stocking stitch; it is possible to use it on garter stitch and ribs, although it is less common. In our example we have used pieces knitted in stocking stitch.

When working Kitchener stitch, your aim is to re-create a knitted row using a sewing needle and yarn that will join two pieces together. Before you start, take a little time to examine just how a knitted fabric works: follow a row of knitting across the knitted piece, looking at how the strand of yarn weaves its way from the beginning to the end of the row.

1   When your knitted piece is complete, do not cast off. Leave the stitches on the needles, ensuring that both needles hold the same number of stitches and that the needle points face to the right with one needle sitting just below the other. Make sure that the working yarn leads from the back needle. Cut the yarn, leaving a long enough tail to complete one row of knitting on your number of stitches plus a little extra. For sock toes 40cm will be plenty.

2   Thread a large sewing needle with your yarn and bring it through the centre of the first stitch on the lower needle from right to left, as if you are purling.

3   Insert the needle through the first stitch on the back needle as if knitting, leaving this stitch on the knitting needle.

4   Bringing the yarn under the knitting needles each time, insert the sewing needle through the first stitch

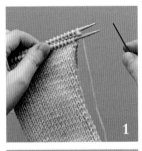

on the lower needle as if to knit, dropping it from the needle as you do so.

5   Insert the sewing needle through the next stitch along to the left as if to purl, leaving it on the knitting needle.

6   Insert the sewing needle through the first stitch on the back needle as if purling, dropping it from the knitting needle as you do so.

7   Insert the sewing needle through the next stitch along to the left as if to knit, leaving it on the knitting needle. Repeat in this manner, working stitches from the lower needle then the back needle, while making sure you achieve a good tension.

When you reach the end of the row and have just one stitch left on each needle, insert the sewing needle through the stitch on the lower knitting needle as if to knit, dropping it from the needle as you do so.

Insert the sewing needle through the final stitch on the remaining needle as if purling, dropping it from the knitting needle as you do so.

8   Once the seam is complete, work along the seam to create an even tension for the stitches by teasing any slack stitches along from the start to the end of the seam.

Joining cast-on and cast-off edges

For some projects you are not required to join two pieces of identical knitting as in the previous example, but are instead required to join a cast-on edge to a cast-off edge.

To do this effectively and without running the risk of dropping stitches, we have suggested that an area of waste yarn is knitted at the beginning and end of the piece. This makes it easy to identify where the piece is to be joined.

As with Kitchener stitch, you will need to sew in an extra row of knitted stitches.

1   Line up the knitted piece so that the cast-on edge and cast-off edge sit horizontally, with the cast-on edge above the cast-off edge.

2   Thread a large sewing needle with the correct colour yarn, making sure you allow plenty of length. Working into the knitted row beneath the waste yarn, insert the needle through the centre of the first stitch on the lower knitted piece from back to front, leaving a tail end of yarn approximately 10cm long.

3   Working into the first knitted row above the waste yarn on the upper piece of knitting, from the front, insert the needle through the knitted piece to the right side of the first stitch and thread the needle back through to the front one stitch along to the left.

4 From the front, insert the needle back into the centre of the first stitch on the lower piece, along to the left by one complete stitch and back up through the centre of the next stitch to the left, making sure that the sewn stitch matches the tension and size of the knitted stitches.

5 Follow the path of the waste yarn, alternating between top and bottom pieces.

6 Continue in this way to the end, making sure that you have exactly mimicked a knitted row and that you have accounted for every stitch on each piece and, of course, changed yarn colour where necessary.

7 Unravel the waste yarn (we love this bit!) and you will have achieved an invisible join between your two knitted pieces.

BEYOND THE BASICS
Woolly Wormhead

To do reverse stocking stitch, we reverse the graft for stocking stitch, by switching the order of the movements:

1 Front needle – insert the needle purlwise, pull the yarn through then slip the loop off the needle.

2 Front needle – insert the needle knitwise, pull the yarn through but leave the loop on the needle.

3 Back needle – insert the needle knitwise, pull the yarn through then slip the loop off the needle.

4 Back needle – insert the needle purlwise, pull the yarn through but leave the loop on the needle.

When looking at the steps taken in these two versions of Kitchener, you can see that each repeat is made up of four movements, which will be referred to as the four elements. And to help understand how you can graft other combinations of stitches, let's look at them a little more closely. The elements are worked in pairs, the first pair on the first (front) needle, and the second pair on the second (back) needle. The four elements for stocking stitch are:

Element 1 Insert needle knitwise, slip loop off needle.
Element 2 Insert needle purlwise, leave loop on needle.
Element 3 Insert needle purlwise, slip loop off needle.
Element 4 Insert needle knitwise, leave loop on needle.

However we combine these four elements and whatever stitches we're trying to create, there are some rules to bear in mind. First, for the sake of simplifying things, always work on the front needle (or facing piece of knitting) first. If you don't do this, you'll quickly get in an awful mess. Second, the first movement of each pair will result in that stitch being slipped off the needle, and the second stitch in each pair will always stay on the needle. There's a good reason for this, which we will look at later.

Now that you know that you can combine the four elements in a different order, let's put it into practice. Rather than try to get our heads around which is the right and wrong side of a stitch that looks virtually identical on both sides, it's easier to use other descriptors to differentiate them. When you've just knitted a row of regular garter stitch (knit every row when working flat), you've created a row of Vs. Now here's the interesting thing – when you're knitting garter stitch you might think that you're creating a series of bumps, but you're not – instead you're creating a series of bumps and Vs.

That row of Vs you've just made by knitting across the row is important. The line of bumps that we're expecting from garter stitch is sitting low at the base of the new stitches you've just created; it's not sitting next to the needle. What you've got on the needle is the top of the Vs. If you flip your knitting over and look at the back of the row you've just knitted, you'll see that the line of bumps is sitting high – it's butted up against the needle. And then you realise the wonder that is garter stitch and how we can graft it. Technically, reverse garter stitch is purling every row, and the front of the work, after completing a row of purl stitches, would have the line of bumps high against the needle, and the bumps would be low on the back of the work.

Avoiding confusion

It's easy to get muddled over opposite terms, and referring to garter stitch and reverse garter stitch is still going to be problematic. Here's where the descriptors will help us – let's call right-side garter stitch 'ridge low' and wrong-side garter stitch 'ridge high'.

When setting up your graft for garter stitch, there's one more thing to take into account. Kitchener stitch is the equivalent of one row of knitting. It doesn't just join two pieces of live knitting; it actually makes a row that connects the live stitches. It's not really an issue with stocking stitch or reverse stocking stitch, as the sides of the work are equal and opposite. But for just about any other stitch, you need to take this into account.

You could bring the wrong sides of the work together and have the right sides facing out, just like with stocking stitch, but there has to be a row missing between them. And in the case of garter stitch that means the back needle needs to be ridge high facing outwards.

To graft ridge low (right-side) garter stitch, we use the four elements in a different order.

For grafting ridge low garter stitch, the front needle (shown here as the bottom needle, **1**) has the ridges low, the back needle (shown here as the top needle, **2**) has them high – right sides of work showing.

5   Front needle – insert the needle purlwise, pull the yarn through then slip the loop off the needle.

6   Front needle – insert the needle knitwise, pull the yarn through but leave the loop on the needle.

7   Back needle – insert the needle purlwise, pull the yarn through then slip the loop off the needle.

8   Back needle – insert the needle knitwise, pull the yarn through but leave the loop on the needle.

Just as reverse stocking stitch Kitchener is the reverse of stocking stitch, we reverse the movements for ridge high garter stitch. To graft ridge high garter stitch, the front needle (shown here as the bottom needle, **3**) has the ridges high, the back needle (shown here as the top needle, **4**) has them low – right sides of work showing.

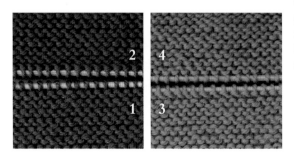

9 Front needle – insert the needle knitwise, pull the yarn through then slip the loop off the needle.

10 Front needle – insert the needle purlwise, pull the yarn through but leave the loop on the needle.

11 Back needle – insert the needle knitwise, pull the yarn through then slip the loop off the needle.

12 Back needle – insert the needle purlwise, pull the yarn through but leave the loop on the needle.

Notice how the garter stitch Kitchener varies from that of the stocking stitch. When you're grafting stocking stitch, or even reverse stocking stitch for that matter, whatever you do on the front needle, you do the opposite on the back needle. When grafting garter stitch, whether it be ridge high or ridge low, you do the same on the back needle as you do on the front.

Adapting to other stitches

To help adapt Kitchener stitch for other stitch patterns and combinations, it helps to understand a little more about how it works. Each time you repeat the four elements, you create a new stitch, only it's not as it seems at first. What you're really doing is creating two halves of a stitch: the latter half of the previous stitch and the first half of the next.

Remember how after the first step on each needle, elements 1 and 3, we drop the loop off the needle? It wouldn't be logical to do that halfway through a new stitch – it makes sense to drop the loop off at the end of creating the stitch, just as you would do with your regular knitting. So, steps 1 and 3 complete the stitch, and steps 2 and 4 set you up for the next stitch.

Now consider the selvedge stitches – the edges of your work. Whenever you read a tutorial for grafting (normally stocking stitch), you'll notice that the first steps you do, right at the beginning of the graft, are actually steps 2 and 4 of the repeat, the two elements that leave the loops on the needle, and the very last steps are steps 1 and 3, the elements where the loop is dropped off the needle. These form the selvedges, and whatever stitch you're grafting, you'll always start the graft with steps 2 and 4, and end it with steps 1 and 3.

Knowing that Kitchener stitch is much more than grafting stocking stitch, and knowing how the four elements work and how they can be combined, allows us to start thinking about how we can graft other stitch patterns. As you've seen, there are rules to follow, and as long as you stick to those rules, you can truly conquer grafting for any stitch.

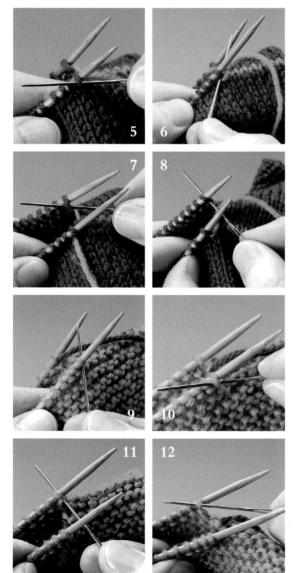

CLIMBING MISTLETOE SOCKS
Jon Dunn-Ballam

This toe-up design with a gently twisting motif is the perfect festive sock.

These socks by Jon Dunn-Ballam are perfect for a Christmas gift, with their motif of twisting mistletoe. They are knitted from the toe up, and on slightly larger needles than your average sock – this provides more comfort and a more relaxed fit for those comfortable winter nights in front of the fire, Jon says. The left and right are worked slightly differently (for the climbing direction of the mistletoe) and differences are marked throughout the pattern. They also incorporate Judy's 'Magic Cast On' technique for a seamless toe. For more on this technique, see page 36. For a photograph of the socks see page 138.

SIZE
To fit ankle/foot circumference 20–25cm (8–10in) (pattern is very stretchy)
Foot length can be adjusted within the pattern

YARN
Easyknits Cherish (4ply weight; 80% superwash merino, 10% cashmere, 10% nylon; 400m/100g skeins)
Apple Daquery 1 x 100g skein
Extra-large socks may require more yarn

NEEDLES
1 set 3mm (UK 11/US 3) circular needles, 80–100cm long (working using 'Magic Loop' method), or set of double-pointed needles in same size

TENSION
30 sts and 44 rows to 10cm over st st using 3mm needles
Mistletoe panel meas 6.5cm across unstretched and 9cm across when gently stretched

SPECIAL ABBREVIATIONS
MB: Make bobble by working (K, P, K, P, K) into 1 stitch, turn, P2tog, P1, P2tog, turn, K3tog
Sl 1P: Slip 1 st purlwise

PATTERN NOTES
The left and right socks are worked slightly differently as the mistletoe pattern is mirrored on each sock

---

Mistletoe pattern

Worked over 23 sts.
Rnd 1: K3, K2tog, K3, yo, P7, yo, K3, SSK, K3.
Rnd 2, 4, 6 & 8: K8, P7, K8.
Rnd 3: K2, K2tog, K3, yo, K1, P3, MB, P3, K1, yo, K3, SSK, K2.
Rnd 5: K1, K2tog, K3, yo, K2, P2, MB, P1, MB, P2, K2, yo, K3, SSK, K1.
Rnd 7: K2tog, K3, yo, K3, P3, MB, P3, K3, yo, K3, SSK.

Left sock

Using 3mm needles and 'Judy's Magic Cast On' for a seamless toe (see page 36), cast on 28 sts (14 instep and 14 sole sts).
Work increases as follows:
Rnd 1:
Instep: K1, M1, knit to last stitch, M1, K1.
Sole: K1, M1, knit to last stitch, M1, K1.
Rnd 2: Knit.
Repeat rounds 1 and 2 until you have 60 sts. (30 instep and 30 sole sts.)★

Foot
Work Mistletoe pattern over first 23 sts and knit remaining sts in the round. Placing stitch markers each side of the Mistletoe pattern may be helpful.

★★Repeat the Mistletoe pattern until you are just more than 3cm short of the back of the heel.

Reverse heel band

Work across the instep sts in pattern to set up for heel band.

K20 sole sts (of the sole sts) and turn.

P10 sole sts (of the sole sts) and turn.

Work across ONLY these centre 10 sts as follows:

Row 1: Sl 1, knit to end, turn.

Row 2: Sl 1P, purl to end, turn.

Repeat these two rows until you have 10 slipped stitches either side of your centre 'band' ending with a purl side row.

Pick up and knit 10 sts down the right side of your band, turn.

Pick up and make a stitch from the gap between your band and the last of the sole stitches, and purl together with the nearest of those remaining sts on the last, turn.

Next row: Knit across picked-up sts and then pick up the remaining 10 sts on the left of the heel band, repeating the picking up and making of a stitch from the gap and knit it together with the nearest stitch on the first third of your sole sts, turn.

Next row: Sl 1P, purl to last stitch before gap (the gap shows between the band and the remaining sole stitches) purl the last stitch before the gap together with the first stitch after the gap, turn.

Next row: Sl 1, knit to last stitch before gap knit the last stitch before the gap together with the first stitch after the gap.

Repeat the last 2 rows until you have worked back down to 30 sts on the sole of the sock.

Return to working in the round and complete two more repeats of the mistletoe pattern before beginning the climbing around the leg.

Left leg

M1, work mistletoe pattern, SSK, knit to end of round.

Repeat this (M1 before, SSK) after the mistletoe pattern every round – this will cause the pattern to spiral around the leg in a clockwise direction.

You will have to shift stitches across needles to be able to work the pattern correctly as it spirals around the leg, making sure you have enough stitches after the patt to work the SSK.

★★★Work as many repeats as you wish until the sock reaches a comfortable length (or if you divided your yarn equally between both socks, until you are almost running short of yarn). The photographed sock on page 138 shows eight repeats.

Cuff

Work a K1 tbl, P1 ribbing, continuing to work the mistletoe pattern throughout so as it breaks through the ribbing itself, work two final repeats of the mistletoe pattern with rib, before casting off.

Cast off

For a toe-up sock, the most difficult part is finding a suitably stretchy cuff that gives the wearer enough ease to get the sock on, without being too loose to stay up. Jon's favourite is one mentioned in Cat Bordhi's book, *Personal Footprints*, and is known as Jeny's Surprisingly Stretchy Bind-Off. It is worked the same way as a basic K2, pass first stitch over second method for casting off but with a little extra.

Working in pattern (knitting all knit and purling all purl stitches) BEFORE every stitch you wish to cast off add a yarn over.

For knit stitches use a backward yarn over and for purl stitches, use a normal yarn over.

When you come to pass the 1st stitch over the 2nd, take the yarn over with the stitch.

There is a great video tutorial on this technique at www.tiny.cc/stretchycastoff

Right sock

Work as for Left Sock to ★.

Set mistletoe patt as foll: K7, work mistletoe pattern, knit remaining sts in the round. Place stitch markers to help keep pattern in correct place.

Work from ★★ on Left Sock to Left Leg heading.

Right leg

Knit to 2 sts before mistletoe pattern, K2tog, mistletoe pattern, M1.

Repeat this (K2tog before, M1) after the mistletoe pattern on every round – this will cause the pattern to spiral around the leg in an anticlockwise direction.

Move sts as necessary to be able to work patt correctly as it spirals round the leg.

Complete as for Left Sock from ★★★. Then weave in all ends and block gently.

13 CREATING CURVES

Create pleasing slopes and curves in your knitted pieces, and avoid stepped edges with this simple but effective technique.

SHORT-ROW SHAPING
Jane Crowfoot

If you've ever knitted socks or a shawl collar cardigan, you may have come across short-row shaping. This technique is used to 'turn' the heel of a sock and to give more fabric in the back of a shawl collar to enable the collar to lie correctly around the neckline.

The technique of working turning rows (as it is also referred to) can be used in many other ways, however. It can form the basis of the design of a piece, as in the Charleston Cushions shown left (pattern on page 150), where slices of knitted colourwork are created using short-rowing rather than the intarsia technique.

This method is also a fantastic way of finishing stepped shoulder seems and creating a shaped bottom edge.

Short-row shaping on a shoulder seam

If you tend to knit women's garments with a set-in or 'shirt' style sleeve, invariably you'll find that you are asked to cast off the shoulder seam in three stages, thus creating three steps in your knitting. On a garment you will create one shoulder seam that slopes to the left and one that slopes to the right.

The samples that we have knitted in red show how both slopes would look **(1)**. These samples have 3 steps each of 7 stitches. We have created the samples in stocking stitch. This technique works for most stitches except garter stitch.

The key things to remember when trying to master this technique are:
- Follow the instructions exactly – however 'wrong' you may think they feel.
- Don't panic in the middle of a row!

When following a knitting pattern you divide for neck shaping and work the left side of the neck first. The first sample then will create a slope to the left.

To work a sample 'shoulder', cast on 21 sts using your preferred yarn and the correct size knitting needles. Work at least 10 rows in stocking stitch ending with wrong side facing.

2 Purl to the last 7 stitches. Keeping the yarn to the side of the work facing you, slip the next stitch from the left needle purlwise onto the right needle.

3 Take the yarn back between the needles as if you are going to knit a stitch.

4 Slip the first stitch on the right needle back to the left needle purlwise so that you don't twist it.

5 Turn your work. Take the yarn to the reverse of the work between both needles. You will see that you have wrapped your yarn around the base of the slipped stitch. Knit to the end of the row.

6 When you look at your knitting on the needle it will look like you have created a hole between the sixth and seventh stitches, and that you also have what looks a little like a purl stitch on the seventh stitch. This is correct, so don't worry if it seems odd.

You are now going to repeat the last 5 steps once more; however, this time you will purl up to the last 14 stitches instead of the last 7 on step 2. Your knitting should look like the sample pictured.

You are now going to complete your final row. With wrong side facing purl the first 7 stitches. You will see that the next stitch has the yarn wrapped around it.

7 Using the right-hand needle, pick up the far side of the wrapped yarn. Place the wrap on the left-hand needle.

8 Purl these two yarns together to create just 1 stitch. This will drop the wrap yarn to the reverse of the work. Purl along to the next wrap stitch and repeat from step 7. Purl to the end of the row.

9 You should now be able to see that you have created a slope in your knitting.

When following a knitting pattern you divide for neck shaping and work the left side of the neck first. You will then be asked to either cast off or put your central stitches onto a holder, before working the other side of the neck. The second sample then will create a slope to the right.

Cast on 21 sts using your preferred yarn. Work at least 10 rows in stocking stitch ending with wrong side facing.

10 Knit to the last 7 stitches. Bring the yarn forward between the two needles as if you are going to purl.

11 Slip the next stitch purlwise from the left needle onto the right.

12 Take the yarn back between the needles as if you are going to knit a stitch.

13 Slip the first stitch on the right needle back to the left needle purlwise so that you don't twist it.

14 Turn your work, keeping the yarn to the facing side of the work. You will see that you have wrapped your yarn around the base of the slipped stitch. Purl to the end of the row.

15 As before, when you look at your knitting on the needle it will look like you have created a hole between the sixth and seventh stitches and that you also have what looks a little like a purl stitch on the seventh stitch.

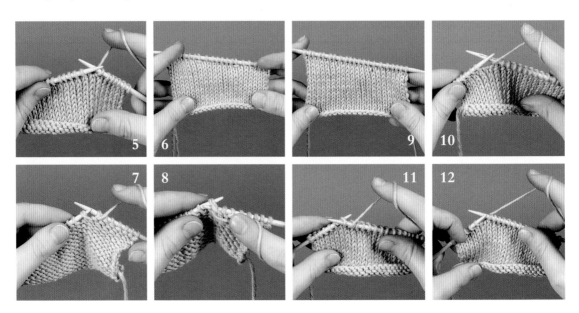

You are now going to repeat from step 10 once more; however, this time you will knit up to the last 14 stitches instead of the last 7 on the first row.

You are now going to complete your final row. With right side facing knit the first 7 stitches. You will see that the next stitch has the yarn wrapped around it.

16 Using the right needle, pick up the front side of the wrapped yarn. In the same movement put your right needle through the next stitch on the left needle in the usual way to knit. Knit these two yarns together to create just 1 stitch. This will drop the wrap yarn to the reverse of the work.

17 Knit along to the next wrap stitch and repeat from step 16. Knit to the end of the row. You should now be able to see that you have created a slope in your knitting.

Converting from stepped seams to short-row shaping

If you want to use the short-row shaping method to shape a shoulder seam, you'll need to start your shaping a row earlier than the pattern tells you to.

For a three-step shoulder seam, work the back of the garment as for the samples above, adding in the stitch counts from the pattern where appropriate.

You will find that you can usually only work 3 steps (one from one shoulder and two from another) before you have to divide for the back of the neck.

For the front of your garment, follow the instructions as for the samples above, replacing the stitch count of 7 stitches with the correct number for your pattern.

Creating a curve

You can use short-row shaping not only to create slopes, but also curves. This is a great technique for shaping the bottom edge of garments **(18)**.

Cast on 40 sts using your preferred yarn. Work 2 rows in stocking stitch beginning with a knit row and ending with wrong side facing.

Next row:
Knit to last 15 sts, wrap st, turn.
Purl to last 15 sts, wrap st, turn.
Knit to last 10 sts, making sure that you deal with the wrap stitch on the 15th stitch from the end, wrap st, turn.

Purl to last 10 sts, making sure that you deal with the wrap stitch on the 15th stitch from the end, wrap st, turn.

Knit to last 5 sts, making sure that you deal with the wrap stitch on the 10th stitch from the end, wrap st, turn.

Purl to last 5 sts, making sure that you deal with the wrap stitch on the 10th stitch from the end, wrap st, turn.

Knit to end, making sure that you deal with the wrap stitch on the 5th stitch from the end, turn.

Purl to end, making sure that you deal with the wrap stitch on the 5th stitch from the end.

Continue in stocking stitch for the required length.

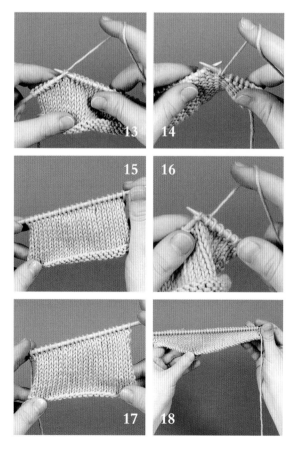

CHARLESTON CUSHIONS
Belinda Boaden

These vibrant cushions and bolster use short-row shaping for a striking effect.

Our delightful cushions and bolster, cleverly worked using short-row shaping, have been designed by Belinda Boaden and were inspired by the gardens of Charleston House in Sussex, the home of the Bloomsbury Group of artists in the 1920s.

The colourways look wonderful on their own and also coordinate beautifully with each other, so you could try your hand at one cushion for your sofa or the whole set.

'I wanted to play around with short rows and produce a pattern that people would enjoy knitting,' says Belinda. 'It's not so important with this design to worry about following the pattern exactly – it really won't matter if you do one wrap-and-turn 1 or 2 stitches before you should, or if you do a stitch the wrong colour in the Fair Isle!'

Belinda has used Jawoll Superwash yarn from Lang. 'It's very good for Fair Isle as it's quite springy and evens out beautifully when steamed, also it's machine-washable which is ideal for cushions,' she says.

'The front piece of the cushion doesn't come out square due to the short rows, but it really doesn't matter once it is sewn up and stuffed with a pad,' adds Belinda.

SIZE
Cushions: 40cm x 40cm (16in x 16in) cushion pad
Bolster: 17cm (6¾in) diameter x 45cm (17¾in) long pad

YARN
Lang Yarns Jawoll Superwash (75% wool, 18% nylon, 7% acrylic; 210m/50g balls)

SHADE	CUSHION 1	CUSHION 2	BOLSTER	ALL 3	
Ecru (83.0094)	2(A)	1	1	4	x 50g balls
Leaf Green (83.0116)	1	2(A)	1	2	x 50g balls
Teal (83.0088)	1	0	1	1	x 50g balls
Green (83.0198)	1	0	1	2	x 50g balls
Yellow (83.0043)	1	1	1	2	x 50g balls
Cerise Pink (83.0184)	1	1	1	1	x 50g balls
Purple (83.0190)	0	1	1	1	x 50g balls

NEEDLES
1 pair 2.75mm (UK 12/US 2) knitting needles
1 pair 3mm (UK 11/US 3) knitting needles

ACCESSORIES
Buttons: 5 per cushion (approx 15mm); 9 per bolster (approx 7mm) with 2 optional end buttons (approx 25mm). (We used Krackled Buttons for the cushions, vintage glass buttons and 2 large vintage Czech glass buttons for the bolster.)
Tapestry needle, pins

TENSION
36 sts and 36 rows to 10cm over Fair Isle pattern using 3mm needles
28 sts and 39 rows to 10cm over striped st st pattern using 3mm needles

SPECIAL ABBREVIATIONS
w&t: Wrap and turn. On a knit row, bring yarn to front of work, slip next stitch, take yarn to back of work, slip wrapped stitch back to left-hand needle. Turn work. If on a purl row, take yarn to back of work, slip next stitch, bring yarn to front of work, slip wrapped stitch back to LH needle, turn work.

Cushions 1 and 2 front

Using 3mm needles and yarn A cast on 144 stitches. Working from chart 1 for either cushion 1 or 2, work 12 rows, repeating pattern as necessary across row.

*Knit 2 rows in yarn A (creates 1 garter ridge). Now change to Chart 2 for appropriate cushion, and work short-row Fair Isle pattern as foll:

Sections 1 and 2

Row 1 (RS): Work 72 sts in patt, wt.
Row 2 and all WS rows: Work in pattern to end.
Row 3: Work 64 sts in patt, w&t.
Row 5: Work 56 sts in patt, w&t.
Row 7: Work 48 sts in patt, w&t.
Row 9: Work 40 sts in patt, w&t.
Row 11: Work 32 sts in patt, w&t.
Row 13: Work 24 sts in patt, w&t.
Rows 15–30 inclusive: As chart, working across all 144 stitches.

Break yarn at the end of the row, and slip stitches from left-hand needle to right-hand needle in order to start next row as a WS row.

Section 3

Begin second Fair Isle section, working again from chart 2, starting with row 1 as a WS row:
Row 1 (WS): Work 24 sts in patt, w&t.
Row 2 (and all RS rows): Work in pattern to end.
Row 3: Work 32 sts in patt, w&t.
Row 5: Work 40 sts, w&t.
Row 7: Work 48 sts, w&t.
Row 9: Work 56 sts, w&t.
Row 11: Work 64 sts, w&t.
Row 13: Work 72 sts, w&t.
Rows 15 and 16: Knit all stitches in yarn A, working wraps with wrapped stitches on row 15.

Section 4

Row 17 (WS): Work 72 sts (chart 2), w&t.
Row 18 (and all RS rows): Work in patt to end.
Row 19: Work 64 sts, w&t.
Row 21: Work 56 sts, w&t.
Row 23: Work 48 sts, w&t.
Row 25: Work 40 sts, w&t.
Row 27: Work 32 sts, w&t.
Row 29: Work 24 sts, w&t.

Row 30: Knit across all stitches in yarn A, working wraps with wrapped stitches.
Additional row (WS): Purl all sts using yarn A.

Section 5

Rows 1–16 inclusive: Work from chart 2 across all 144 stitches (row 1 will be RS).

Section 6

Row 17 (RS): Work 72 sts (Chart 2), w&t.
Row 18 (and all WS rows): Work in pattern to end.
Row 19: Work 64 sts, w&t.
Row 21: Work 56 sts, w&t.
Row 23: Work 48 sts, w&t.
Row 25: Work 40 sts, w&t.
Row 27: Work 32 sts, w&t.
Row 29: Work 24 sts, w&t.
Row 30: Knit 24 sts using yarn A.

Repeat from * once more, then work 12 rows in stocking stitch, across all sts, from Chart 3 for appropriate cushion. Cast off.

Cushion 1 back

Lower back

Using 2.75mm needles and Green cast on 111 stitches . Work 18 rows in garter st. Change to 3mm needles and continue in stocking st stripe pattern from Chart 4, until piece measures 24cm. Cast off.

Upper back

Using 2.75mm needles and Green cast on 111 stitches, work 10 rows in garter st. Work buttonholes as foll:

Next row: K16, ★Sl 1 purlwise, yfwd and leave at the front, Sl 1 purlwise, pass 1st slipped stitch over 2nd, Sl 1 purlwise, pass 2nd slipped stitch over 3rd, Sl 1 purlwise, pass 3rd slipped stitch over 4th. Put 4th stitch on left needle, reversing it.

Reverse, twist or turn last stitch on RH needle. Pull yarn tightly, lay over RH needle from front to back and pass the turned stitch over it. Make 4 firm backward loops onto RH needle, K2tog, K14. Repeat from ★ across row, making 5 buttonholes.

Work 7 more rows in garter st. Change to 3mm needles and continue in stocking st stripe pattern from Chart 4, until piece measures 24cm. Cast off.

Cushion 2 back

Lower back

Using 2.75mm needles and shade Cerise Pink cast on 111 stitches. Work 18 rows in garter st. Change to 3mm needles and continue in stocking st stripe pattern from Chart 4, until piece meas 24cm. Cast off.

Upper back

Using 2.75mm needles and Cerise Pink cast on 111 stitches. Work 10 rows in garter st. Work buttonholes as for Cushion 1, followed by 7 more rows of garter st. Complete in stripe pattern from Chart 4, until piece meas 24cm, Cast off.

Making up

Block pieces lightly, following instructions on ball band. Overlap buttonhole band over button band, place the two back pieces onto the front, wrong sides together, and pin in place. Mattress stitch backs to front. Sew on buttons to correspond with buttonholes and weave in all ends.

Bolster

The bolster has two different coloured ends, but alternatively you could make them matching.

Ends

Knit one end in each of the cushion colourways. Using 3mm needles and yarn A cast on 32 stitches.

★Knit 2 rows (making 1 garter ridge). Now work pattern from Chart 2 for appropriate cushion, shaping short-row Fair Isle pattern as foll:

Sections 1 and 2

Row 1: Work 28 sts in patt, w&t.
Row 2 (and all WS rows to 14): Work in pattern to end.
Row 3: Work 24 sts, w&t.
Row 5: Work 20 sts, w&t.
Row 7: Work 16 sts, w&t.
Row 9: Work 12 sts, w&t.
Row 11: Work 8 sts, w&t.
Row 13: Work 4 sts, w&t.
Rows 15 and 16: From chart, working all stitches and wraps with wrapped stitches.
Row 17: Work 28 sts, w&t.
Row 18 (and all WS rows): Work in pattern to end.
Row19: Work 24 sts, w&t.
Row 21: Work 20 sts, w&t.
Row 23: Work 16 sts, w&t.
Row 25: Work 12 sts, w&t.
Row 27: Work 8 sts, w&t.
Row 29: Work 4 sts, w&t.
Row 30: Work in pattern to end.
Pattern repeats from ★ working all stitches and wraps with wrapped stitches on first knit row. Repeat these 32 rows 6 more times so that piece forms a circle. Cast off.

Side

Using 2.75mm needles and Ecru cast on 127 stitches. Work 18 rows in garter st.

Change to 3mm needles and continue in stocking st stripe pattern from Chart 5. Repeat the stripes until piece meas 53cm.

Change to shade Ecru and 2.75mm needles and work 10 rows in garter st.

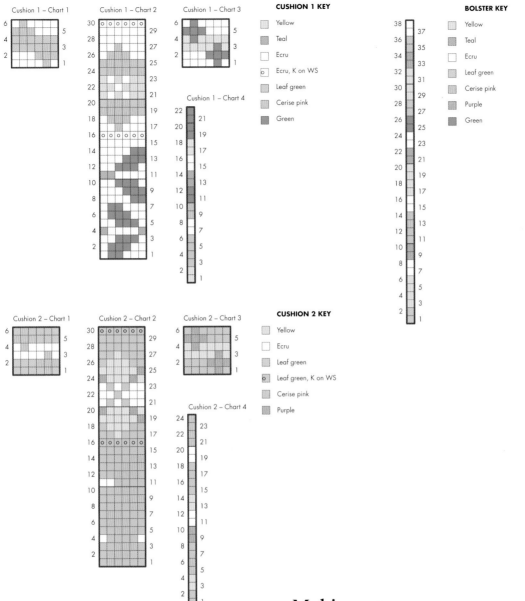

Cushion 1 – Chart 1

Cushion 1 – Chart 2

Cushion 1 – Chart 3

Cushion 1 – Chart 4

CUSHION 1 KEY

	Yellow
	Teal
	Ecru
⊙	Ecru, K on WS
	Leaf green
	Cerise pink
	Green

BOLSTER KEY

	Yellow
	Teal
	Ecru
	Leaf green
	Cerise pink
	Purple
	Green

Cushion 2 – Chart 1

Cushion 2 – Chart 2

Cushion 2 – Chart 3

Cushion 2 – Chart 4

CUSHION 2 KEY

	Yellow
	Ecru
	Leaf green
⊙	Leaf green, K on WS
	Cerise pink
	Purple

Work buttonhole row as foll:

Next row: K10, ★Sl 1 purlwise, yfwd and leave at the front, Sl 1 purlwise, pass 1st slipped stitch over 2nd, Sl 1 purlwise, pass 2nd slipped stitch over 3rd, put 3rd stitch on left-hand needle, reversing it.

Reverse, twist or turn last stitch on RH needle. Pull yarn tightly, lay over RH needle from front to back and pass the turned stitch over it. Make 3 firm backward loops onto RH needle, K2tog, K9. Repeat from ★ across row, making 9 buttonholes.

Work 8 more rows in garter st, ending with WS facing. Cast off.

Making up

Block pieces lightly, according to instructions on ball band. Thread a double thickness of yarn along the inside edge of the end pieces and draw up tightly to close. Stitch the cast-on and cast-off edges together to close the circle.

Overlap the buttonhole band end of the main piece over the button band and pin in place. Pin each end piece in place at the ends of the main piece and mattress stitch into place. Sew buttons onto button band to correspond to buttonholes and large buttons onto centre of end pieces. Weave in all ends.

HOLDING THE NEEDLES & YARN

Holding the needles is one of the toughest things to master in knitting, so if you find it hard, don't be put off – it gets easier after this. How you hold the needles will depend on how you plan to knit, but you may not know that yet. You can hold the yarn in your right or left hand. If you hold it in your right hand, that is the British way; if you hold it in your left hand then that is the Continental way of knitting. Though awkward at first, holding the needles either way becomes much more comfortable with practice. Have a go at both methods and you will quickly find out which one is most suitable for you.

The English method

This is the most commonly used method in the UK and US. The needles are held differently in the right and left hands.

1. Hold the needle with the stitches on in your left hand. Wrap the yarn around the little finger of your right hand and then come up between your index and second fingers.

2. Hold the other needle in your right hand, placing it in the crook between the thumb and index finger, in the same way as you would hold a pencil. The right-hand index finger is going to control the tension of the yarn, so it is important to keep the yarn slightly taut around this finger.

The Scottish method

As the name suggests, this way of holding the yarn and needles originated in the north of Britain. Some knitters tuck the end of the right-hand needle under their arm when using this method.

1. Hold the needle with the stitches on in your left hand. Wrap the yarn around the little finger of your right hand and then come up between your index and second fingers.

2. Hold the other needle in your right hand, placing your hand on top of the needle, in the same way as you would hold a knife. The right-hand index finger is going to control the tension of the yarn, so it is important to keep the yarn around this finger slightly taut.

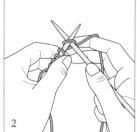

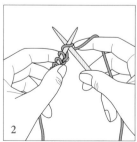

The Continental method

This method is the most popular in Continental Europe. It is also a technique that many left-handers find easy to use if they are knitting right-handed.

1   Hold the needle with the stitches on in your right hand. Wrap the yarn around the little finger and then around the index finger of your left hand. Then move the needle with the stitches on into your left hand.

2   Hold the other needle in your right hand, holding it from above. The tension of the yarn will be controlled by your left-hand index finger, so it is important to keep the yarn around it slightly taut.

Left-handed method

Obviously this is probably the most suitable method if you are left-handed, though as all knitting techniques involve using both hands, many left-handers have no problem with right-handed techniques.

1   Hold the needle with the stitches on in your right hand. Wrap the yarn around the little finger and then around the index finger of your left hand.

2   Hold the other needle in your left hand, holding it from above. The tension will be controlled by your left-hand index finger, so it is important to keep the yarn around it slightly taut.

Perfecting your technique

Once you are able to control the needles, ignore them for a while and learn to knit. You can perfect your holding technique afterwards.

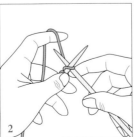

STANDARD YARN WEIGHT SYSTEM

Yarn weight symbol & category names	LACE (0)	SUPER FINE (1)	FINE (2)	LIGHT (3)	MEDIUM (4)	BULKY (5)	SUPER BULKY (6)
Type of yarns in category	Fingering 10-count crochet thread, 2ply	Sock, Fingering, Baby, 4ply	Sport, Baby, Heavy 4ply	DK, Light Worsted	Worsted, Afghan, Aran	Chunky, Craft, Rug	Bulky, Roving, Super Chunky
Knit tension range in stocking stitch to 10cm	33–40** sts	27–32 sts	23–26 sts	21–24 st	16–20 sts	12–15 sts	6–11 sts
Recommended needle in metric size range	1.5–2.25 mm	2.25–3.25 mm	3.25–3.75 mm	3.75–4.5 mm	4.5–5.5 mm	5.5–8 mm	8 mm and larger
Recommended needle US size range	000–1	1 to 3	3 to 5	5 to 7	7 to 9	9 to 11	11and larger
Crochet tension* ranges in double crochet to 10cm	32–42 double crochets**	21–32 sts	16–20 sts	12–17 sts	11–14 sts	8–11 sts	5–9 sts
Recommended hook in metric size range	Steel*** 1.6–1.4 mm	2.25 –3.5 mm	3.5 –4.5 mm	4.5 –5.5 mm	5.5 –6.5 mm	6.5 –9 mm	9 mm and larger
Recommended hook US size range Steel***	6, 7, 8 Regular hook B–1	B–1 to E–4	E–4 to 7	7 to I–9	I–9 to K–10 ½	K–10 ½ to M–13	M–13 and larger

* GUIDELINES ONLY: The above reflect the most commonly used gauges and needle or hook sizes for specific yarn categories.

** Lace weight yarns are usually knitted or crocheted on larger needles and hooks to create lacy, openwork patterns. Accordingly, a gauge range is difficult to determine. Always follow the gauge stated in your pattern.

*** Steel crochet hooks are sized differently from regular hooks—the higher the number, the smaller the hook, which is the reverse of regular hook sizing

Source: Craft Yarn Council

ABBREVIATIONS
& NEEDLE SIZES

Knitting Needle Sizes

Millimetre range . . . . US size

Millimetre range	US size
2.25mm	1
2.75mm	2
3.25mm	3
3.5mm	4
3.75mm	5
4mm	6
4.5mm	7
5mm	8
5.5mm	9
6mm	10
6.5mm	10½
8mm	11
9mm	13
10mm	15
12.75mm	17
15mm	19
19mm	35
25mm	50

Crochet Hook Sizes

Millimetre range . . . . US size*

Millimetre range	US size*
2.25mm	B-1
2.75mm	C-2
3.25mm	D-3
3.5mm	E-4
3.75mm	F-5
4mm	G-6
4.5mm	7
5mm	H-8
5.5mm	I-9
6mm	J-10
6.5mm	K-10½
8mm	L-11
9mm	M/N-13
10mm	N/P-15
15mm	P/Q
16mm	Q
25mm	S

*Letter or number may vary. Rely on the millimeter (mm) sizing.
Source: Craft Yarn Council

Abbreviations

alt	alternate
approx	approximately
beg	begin(ning)
cn	cable needle
cont	continue(ing)
dec	decrease (work 2 stitches together)
DK	double knitting
DPN	double-pointed needle
est	established
foll	follow(s)(ing)
inc	increase(ing)
K	knit
KFB	knit into front and back of stitch
K2tog	knit 2 stitches together
K3tog	knit 3 stitches together
LH	left hand
meas	measures
M1	make one (inc 1 stitch)
MB	make bobble
P	purl

INDEX

Acknowledgements

There are so many wonderful people who have contributed to this book and I owe them all a huge thank you.

To the designers and the masters whose work and dedication to their craft has made this book the amazing work it is; the team at *The Knitter* including Rosee Woodland, Helen Spedding, Jude Curle, Sarah Clark and Jennifer Storey as well as Jen Arnall-Culliford; the photo shoot team, Phil, Jesse, Kimberley, Sarah and Joe as well as Sarah Eastel who we miss terribly – her choice of locations set the scene for our work; the wonderful yarn companies who continue to support *The Knitter*, to Shirish Jain and Knitpro Needles whose superlative needles and crochet hooks are featured throughout; Nicky who organises me and points me in the right direction; to Kerry and Debora for their advice and nurturing; to Amy, Katie and the team at Anova who took me seriously, and finally, to my lovely husband, Paul and my wonderful sons, Joe and Reef, who indulge my obsession with knitting by always wanting new hats, gloves and jumpers.

Whatever the craft, we have the book for you – just head straight to Collins & Brown crafty HeadQuarters!

LoveCrafts is the one-stop destination for all things crafty, with the very latest news and information about all our books and authors. It doesn't stop there...

Enter our fabulous competitions and win great prizes
Download free patterns from our talented authors
Collect LoveCrafts loyalty points and receive special offers on all our books

Join our crafting community at LoveCrafts – we look forward to meeting you!

The Knitter is a monthly magazine aimed at knitters who love quality yarns and beautiful patterns. With inspiration from world-class designers and new techniques to try, *The Knitter* offers an extra level of creativity to crafters. A wide range of original clothing and homeware patterns every issue makes *The Knitter* eminently collectable!

FOR THOSE WHO LOVE TO KNIT

For those who love to knit, KnitPro needles are the top choice. These beautiful and high-quality needles includes the Symfonie Wood, Spectra Acrylic and Nova Metal ranges. With straights, DPNs, circulars and interchangeable circulars available in every range, it's easy to find the perfect needle for any project.